SALESFORCE CERTI

ADMINISTRATOR

EXAM PREP 2024-2025

Over 200+ Practice Questions, detailed Answer Explanations
and Exam Tips.

CAREERCERT PUBLISHING

CAREERCERT PUBLISHING

CAREERCERT PUBLISHING

COPYRIGHT

PREFACE

Welcome to the 1st edition of SALESFORCE CERTIFIED ADMINISTRATOR EXAM PREP 2024-2025 .This book has been meticulously crafted by CareerCert Publishing to support you in your journey toward certification. Whether you are a beginner or an experienced professional, this book is designed to provide comprehensive coverage of the exam objectives and to equip you with the knowledge and skills required to succeed.

At CareerCert Publishing, we understand the importance of certification in advancing your career and achieving your professional goals. Our team of experts, authors, and educators have collaborated to create a resource that is not only informative but also engaging and practical. Each chapter is structured to enhance your understanding of key concepts, and includes practice questions, real-world examples, and test-taking strategies to ensure you are well-prepared for the certification exam.

We are committed to providing the highest quality educational materials, and we continually update our content to reflect the latest industry standards and exam requirements. Your success is our priority, and we hope this book serves as a valuable tool in your preparation.

We would like to express our gratitude to the many individuals who have contributed to this edition. Special thanks to our reviewers for their invaluable feedback, and to our production team for their dedication and hard work.

We wish you the best of luck on your certification journey. Remember, persistence and dedication are key to achieving your goals. Thank you for choosing CareerCert Publishing.

INTRODUCTION

The Salesforce Certified Administrator exam is designed for individuals responsible for configuring, customizing, and managing the Salesforce platform to meet the specific needs of a business. This role typically involves setting up users, customizing the Salesforce interface, managing data, and ensuring system security.

EXAM FORMAT

The exam is a computer-based, multiple-choice test that assesses a candidate's knowledge and skills in Salesforce administration. It consists of 60 questions and must be completed within 105 minutes. To pass, a candidate must achieve a score of 65%.

EXAM TOPICS

The Salesforce Certified Administrator exam covers a wide range of topics, including:

- **Salesforce Administration Fundamentals:** Understanding the Salesforce platform, basic setup, and navigation.
- **Configuration and Customization:** Creating custom objects, fields, page layouts, record types, and workflows.
- **Security and Data Management:** Implementing security controls, managing data integrity, and performing data imports and exports.
- **User Management:** Creating and managing user profiles, roles, and permissions.

Minimum Requirements

There are no formal prerequisites to take the Salesforce Certified Administrator exam. However, Salesforce recommends having at least 6-12 months of hands-on experience as a Salesforce Administrator before attempting the exam. This practical experience is crucial for understanding real-world scenarios and applying knowledge effectively.

Exam Updates

Salesforce regularly updates its certifications to align with platform enhancements. It's essential to check the official Salesforce certification website for the most current information on exam content and format.

Exam Cost

The cost of the Salesforce Certified Administrator exam varies depending on the region. It's recommended to check the official Salesforce website for the exact cost in your location.

Retake Policy

If you don't pass the exam, you can retake it after a waiting period. The retake policy, including the waiting period and any associated fees, is subject to change and can be found on the Salesforce certification website.

Validation and Certificate Validity

Upon passing the exam, Salesforce will validate your achievement and issue a digital certificate. The certificate serves as proof of your expertise in Salesforce administration. The validity of the certification is ongoing, but Salesforce may introduce recertification requirements in the future to ensure that certified professionals stay updated with platform advancements.

BENEFITS OF THE EXAM

Earning a Salesforce Certified Administrator certification offers a multitude of advantages for both individuals and organizations.

Benefits for Individuals

- **Enhanced Career Prospects:** Certification validates your expertise in Salesforce administration, making you a highly sought-after professional in the job market.
- **Increased Earning Potential:** Certified administrators often command higher salaries and have better negotiation power.
- **Skill Development:** The preparation process for the exam helps you develop a deep understanding of the Salesforce platform and its capabilities.
- **Professional Recognition:** Certification establishes you as a credible and knowledgeable Salesforce expert.
- **Career Advancement:** It can serve as a stepping stone to more advanced Salesforce certifications and roles.

Benefits for Organizations

- **Improved Efficiency:** Certified administrators can optimize Salesforce to streamline business processes and increase productivity.
- **Enhanced Data Management:** Effective data management is crucial for business success, and certified administrators excel in this area.
- **Increased User Satisfaction:** By providing efficient and user-friendly Salesforce setups, certified administrators contribute to higher user satisfaction.

- **Reduced Costs:** Efficient Salesforce administration can lead to cost savings through improved data management and reduced errors.
- **Competitive Advantage:** Having certified administrators demonstrates a commitment to leveraging technology for business growth.

SALESFORCE PLATFORM FUNDAMENTALS

Salesforce, a cloud-based customer relationship management (CRM) platform, has revolutionized how businesses interact with their customers. It's a robust system capable of handling everything from sales and marketing to customer service and support. At its core, Salesforce is a multi-tenant architecture, meaning multiple organizations share the same platform infrastructure, but their data is isolated. This model ensures scalability, reliability, and security.

SALESFORCE ARCHITECTURE AND CORE CONCEPTS

Multi-tenant Architecture: Salesforce operates on a multi-tenant architecture. This means that multiple organizations share the same platform infrastructure, but their data is completely segregated. This model offers several advantages:

- **Cost-effectiveness:** Salesforce can achieve economies of scale by serving multiple customers on a single platform.
- **Scalability:** The platform can easily accommodate growing customer needs without requiring significant infrastructure changes.
- **Security:** Salesforce employs robust security measures to protect customer data.

Metadata-Driven: Salesforce is metadata-driven, meaning the structure and definition of your data (objects, fields, relationships, etc.) are stored separately from the actual data. This makes it easier to customize and modify your Salesforce org without affecting the underlying data.

Force.com Platform: This is the underlying platform that powers Salesforce applications. It provides a development environment for building custom applications, integrations, and workflows.

Core Components:

- **Objects:** These are the building blocks of Salesforce data. They represent real-world entities like Accounts, Contacts, Leads, Opportunities, and Cases.
- **Records:** Instances of objects are called records. For example, a specific company would be an Account record.
- **Fields:** Fields define the data stored within an object. For example, an Account object might have fields like Name, Phone, Website, and Industry.
- **Relationships:** Objects can be related to each other through parent-child relationships. This allows you to create complex data models. For example, an Account can have many Contacts.
- **Pages:** Salesforce provides standard pages for viewing and editing records, but you can also create custom pages using Visual force or Lightning App Builder.
- **Profiles and Permission Sets:** These control user access to data and system features. Profiles define a set of permissions, while permission sets can be assigned to grant additional access.

NAVIGATING THE SALESFORCE USER INTERFACE

The Salesforce user interface is designed to be intuitive and user-friendly. The main components include:

- **Navigation Bar:** Located at the top of the page, it provides access to different parts of the application.
- **App Launcher:** This icon allows you to switch between different Salesforce apps.
- **Global Search:** Use this to quickly find records, objects, or other items.
- **Home Page:** This is the default page when you log in. It can be customized to display relevant information.
- **Standard Objects:** These are pre-built objects like Accounts, Contacts, Leads, Opportunities, and Cases.
- **Custom Objects:** You can create custom objects to store specific data not covered by standard objects.
- **Related Lists:** These display related records on a record detail page.

- **Page Layouts:** Control the layout of record detail pages.
- **Tabs:** Organize objects and custom applications into tabs for easy access.

DATA MODEL AND OBJECT RELATIONSHIPS

A well-designed data model is crucial for the effective use of Salesforce. It ensures data integrity, accuracy, and efficiency.

Data Model: This is a logical representation of your organization's data and how it relates. It involves defining objects, fields, and relationships between them.

Object Relationships: Salesforce supports several types of relationships:

- **Master-Detail Relationship:** A strong relationship where the child record depends on the parent record. For example, an Opportunity is related to an Account.
- **Lookup Relationship:** A weaker relationship where the child record can exist independently of the parent record. For example, a Contact can be related to multiple Accounts.
- **Many-to-Many Relationship:** Requires a junction object to relate two objects that have a many-to-many relationship. For example, a Contact can be related to many Campaigns, and a Campaign can have many Contacts.

Best Practices for Data Modeling:

- **Identify key entities:** Determine the essential objects for your business.
- **Define relationships:** Establish how objects relate to each other.
- **Consider data volume:** Optimize data storage and performance.
- **Enforce data integrity:** Implement validation rules and required fields.
- **Standardize data:** Use consistent data formats and values.

UNDERSTANDING SALESFORCE EDITIONS AND LIMITS

Salesforce offers various editions to cater to different business sizes and needs. Each edition has specific features, limits, and pricing.

Key Editions:

- **Essentials:** Basic CRM features for small businesses.
- **Professional:** Expanded features for sales, service, and marketing.
- **Enterprise:** Comprehensive features for complex sales and service processes.
- **Unlimited:** Highest level of features, performance, and support.

Understanding Limits:

Salesforce imposes limits on various aspects to ensure performance and fairness among users. These limits include:

- **Data storage:** The amount of data you can store.
- **Number of records:** The maximum number of records per object.
- **API calls:** The number of API calls allowed.
- **File storage:** The amount of file storage available.
- **Users:** The number of licensed users.

ORGANIZATION SETUP AND MANAGEMENT

A Salesforce organization is your company's instance of the Salesforce platform. It's where you store your data, configure your settings, and manage your users.

Creating a Salesforce Organization:

- **Sign up for a Salesforce account:** You can start with a free trial to explore the platform.
- **Provide organization information:** This includes your company name, address, and other relevant details.
- **Choose an edition:** Select the Salesforce edition that best suits your business needs and budget.
- **Set up initial users:** Add the necessary users to your organization.

Managing a Salesforce Organization:

- **Organization-Wide Defaults:** Establish default settings for various aspects of your organization, such as currency, language, email settings, and data retention policies.
- **Company Information:** Maintain accurate information about your company, including address, phone number, and website.
- **User Management:** Add, edit, and deactivate users as needed.
- **Data Management:** Import, export, and manage your organization's data.
- **Security Settings:** Configure security settings to protect your data and organization.
- **Customization:** Customize the Salesforce interface to match your business processes.

CONFIGURING ORGANIZATION-WIDE DEFAULTS

Organization-wide defaults set the foundation for your Salesforce organization. They apply to all users unless overridden by specific user settings or profiles.

Key Organization-Wide Defaults:

- **Currency:** Set the default currency for your organization.
- **Locale:** Specify the language and regional settings for your users.
- **Email:** Configure email settings for sending and receiving emails within Salesforce.
- **Data Retention:** Determine how long data is retained in your organization.
- **Business Hours:** Define standard business hours for your organization.
- **Case Management:** Set up case escalation rules and other case-related defaults.

MANAGING PROFILES AND PERMISSION SETS

Profiles and permission sets are fundamental to controlling user access in Salesforce.

Profiles:

- Define a set of permissions and settings for a group of users with similar roles.
- Control access to objects, fields, tabs, and other Salesforce features.
- Assign profiles to users when creating or editing their accounts.

Permission Sets:

- Grant additional permissions to users beyond their profile permissions.
- Assign specific objects, fields, and features to users.
- Can be assigned and revoked independently of profiles.

Best Practices:

- Create granular profiles and permission sets to minimize security risks.
- Use permission sets to assign specific permissions to users without modifying their profiles.
- Regularly review and update profiles and permission sets to reflect changes in your organization.

SETTING UP USER LICENSES AND PROFILES

To add users to your Salesforce organization, you need to assign them appropriate licenses and profiles.

User Licenses:

- Determine the type of access users require (e.g., Sales, Service, Platform).
- Assign licenses based on user roles and responsibilities.
- Manage license assignments and renewals.

Profiles:

- Assign profiles to users based on their license type and required permissions.
- Customize profiles to meet specific user needs.
- Ensure proper separation of duties by assigning appropriate permissions.

UNDERSTANDING DATA OWNERSHIP AND SHARING

Data ownership and sharing are critical for maintaining data integrity and security in Salesforce.

Data Ownership:

- Determine who owns each record in your organization.
- Establish clear ownership guidelines to prevent data conflicts.
- Use ownership to control access and sharing.

Data Sharing:

- Define how data is shared among users and groups.
- Use sharing rules, role hierarchies, and organization-wide defaults to control data visibility.
- Balance data accessibility with security requirements.

USER MANAGEMENT AND SECURITY

Creating and Managing Users

Efficient user management is essential for maintaining a secure and productive Salesforce environment.

- **User Creation:** Add new users to your organization, providing necessary information such as name, email, and username.
- **User Activation:** Activate user accounts after creation.
- **User Deactivation:** Deactivate user accounts when employees leave the company or no longer require access.
- **User Information Updates:** Keep user information up-to-date.

Assigning User Roles and Permissions

Properly assigning user roles and permissions is crucial for ensuring data security and efficiency.

- **Role Hierarchy:** Establish a hierarchical structure to define reporting relationships and data access.
- **Profile Assignment:** Assign appropriate profiles to users based on their roles and responsibilities.
- **Permission Set Assignment:** Grant additional permissions using permission sets.
- **Review and Adjust:** Regularly review user roles and permissions to ensure they align with business needs.

IMPLEMENTING SECURITY CONTROLS

Strong security controls protect your Salesforce organization and data.

- **Password Policies:** Enforce complex password requirements, including password length, character types, and expiration policies.
- **Session Settings:** Configure session timeout settings to protect user data.
- **IP Restrictions:** Limit access to Salesforce from specific IP addresses.
- **Two-Factor Authentication (2FA):** Implement 2FA for enhanced security.
- **Data Loss Prevention (DLP):** Prevent sensitive data from being leaked.

Understanding Data Security and Privacy

Protecting sensitive data is paramount in Salesforce.

- **Data Classification:** Categorize data based on sensitivity levels.
- **Encryption:** Encrypt sensitive data to protect it from unauthorized access.
- **Data Masking:** Replace sensitive data with fake values for testing purposes.
- **Privacy Compliance:** Adhere to data privacy regulations (e.g., GDPR, CCPA).

Managing User Interface Customization

Customize the Salesforce user interface to improve user experience and productivity.

- **Page Layouts:** Create custom page layouts to display relevant information for different user roles.
- **Tabs:** Organize objects and custom applications into tabs for easy access.
- **Lightning App Builder:** Build custom Lightning apps to streamline user workflows.
- **Visual force:** Develop custom pages for complex user interfaces.
- **User Preferences:** Allow users to personalize their Salesforce experience.
  By effectively managing your Salesforce organization, users, and security, you can optimize the platform for your business and protect your valuable data.

DATA MANAGEMENT

While Salesforce comes pre-built with standard objects like Accounts, Contacts, and Opportunities, often your business requires specific data that doesn't fit into these molds. This is where custom objects and fields come into play.

Custom Objects:
- **Purpose:** To store information specific to your business needs.
- **Creation:** You can create custom objects through the Object Manager.
- **Fields:** You'll need to define the fields for your custom object. These can be text, number, date, picklist, or other data types.
- **Relationships:** You can relate custom objects to standard objects or other custom objects using master-detail, lookup, or junction object relationships.
- **Best Practices:** Clearly define the purpose of the custom object, keep it simple, and avoid over-complicating your data model.

Custom Fields:
- **Purpose:** To add additional information to standard or custom objects.
- **Types:** Text, number, date, currency, picklist, checkbox, and more.
- **Validation Rules:** You can enforce data quality by setting up validation rules for custom fields.
- **Best Practices:** Use descriptive field labels, consider data types carefully, and avoid excessive fields.

DATA IMPORT AND EXPORT

Salesforce provides various methods to import and export data.

Data Import:
- **Data Import Wizard:** For smaller datasets, the Data Import Wizard is user-friendly.

- **Data Loader:** For larger datasets or more complex imports, Data Loader is a powerful tool.
- **Bulk API:** For programmatic data imports, the Bulk API offers high performance.
- **Considerations:** Data cleaning, matching records, handling duplicates, and setting ownership.

Data Export:

- **Data Export Wizard:** For exporting data to CSV or Excel format.
- **Report Exports:** Exporting data from reports.
- **Data Loader:** For exporting large datasets or specific data formats.
- **Considerations:** Data formatting, export limits, and data privacy.

DATA VALIDATION AND CLEANSING

Maintaining data accuracy is crucial for the success of your Salesforce organization.

Data Validation:

- **Validation Rules:** Define rules to prevent invalid data from being entered.
- **Required Fields:** Ensure critical fields are filled in.
- **Picklist Values:** Restrict data entry to predefined options.
- **Formula Fields:** Calculate values based on other fields.

Data Cleansing:

- **Duplicate Detection:** Identify and merge duplicate records.
- **Data Standardization:** Ensure consistent data formatting.
- **Data Enrichment:** Add missing data through external sources.
- **Data Quality Assessment:** Regularly assess data quality.

DATA QUALITY AND GOVERNANCE

A robust data governance framework ensures data accuracy, consistency, and reliability.

Data Quality:

- **Data Profiling:** Analyze data to identify inconsistencies and errors.
- **Data Cleansing:** Correct data issues.
- **Data Standardization:** Enforce data standards.
- **Data Monitoring:** Continuously monitor data quality.

Data Governance:

- **Data Ownership:** Define data ownership and responsibilities.
- **Data Access Controls:** Implement appropriate access controls.
- **Data Retention Policies:** Determine data retention periods.
- **Data Backup and Recovery:** Establish backup procedures.
- **Data Security:** Protect data from unauthorized access.

MASS DATA UPDATES AND BULK API

For large-scale data modifications, the Bulk API is the preferred method.

Bulk API:

- **High Performance:** Handles large volumes of data efficiently.
- **Asynchronous Processing:** Allows for background data updates.
- **Error Handling:** Provides detailed error information.
- **Use Cases:** Data migration, bulk updates, and data exports.

Mass Data Updates:

- **Data Loader:** Can be used for mass updates, but performance might be limited for large datasets.
- **Apex Triggers:** For programmatic mass updates, but use with caution due to performance implications.
- **Considerations:** Data validation, error handling, and performance optimization.

SALES AND MARKETING APPLICATIONS

Sales Cloud is the heart of Salesforce for sales teams. It provides tools for managing leads, opportunities, accounts, contacts, and sales processes.

Core Features:

- **Lead Management:** Capture and qualify leads.
- **Opportunity Management:** Track sales deals from inception to closure.
- **Account Management:** Manage customer information and relationships.
- **Contact Management:** Maintain contact details and interactions.
- **Sales Forecasting:** Predict sales performance.
- **Sales Process Automation:** Automate repetitive tasks and improve efficiency.

Lead Management and Conversion

Effective lead management is crucial for sales success.

- **Lead Capture:** Collect lead information from various sources (website, email, events).
- **Lead Qualification:** Assess lead quality and prioritize follow-up.
- **Lead Assignment:** Assign leads to sales reps.
- **Lead Conversion:** Convert qualified leads into opportunities.
- **Lead Scoring:** Prioritize leads based on specific criteria.

Opportunity Management and Forecasting

Opportunity management helps sales teams track and close deals effectively.

- **Opportunity Creation:** Create opportunities from qualified leads.
- **Opportunity Stages:** Define the sales pipeline stages.
- **Probability:** Assign probability of closing to each opportunity.
- **Forecasting:** Predict future sales revenue based on opportunity data.
- **Sales Metrics:** Track key sales performance indicators (KPIs).

Sales Process Automation (Workflows, Approvals)

Automate repetitive tasks and improve sales efficiency with workflows and approvals.

- **Workflow Rules:** Automatically execute actions based on record changes.
- **Approval Processes:** Route records for approval based on defined criteria.
- **Process Builder:** Create complex automated processes.
- **Automation Studio:** For more advanced automation, including email marketing.

Campaign Management and Analytics

Measure the effectiveness of your marketing campaigns with Salesforce.

- **Campaign Creation:** Define campaign objectives and target audience.
- **Campaign Member:** Associate leads, contacts, or accounts with campaigns.
- **Campaign Response:** Track campaign responses and conversions.
- **Campaign Analytics:** Measure campaign performance and ROI.

Marketing Automation Basics

Automate marketing tasks to improve efficiency and lead nurturing.

- **Email Marketing:** Send targeted emails to leads and customers.
- **Lead Nurturing:** Guide leads through the sales funnel with personalized content.
- **Marketing Automation Platform:** Integrate with external marketing automation tools.
- **Campaign Optimization:** Continuously refine marketing campaigns based on performance data.

SERVICE AND SUPPORT APPLICATIONS

Salesforce Service Cloud is designed to streamline customer service operations. Its core features are centered around case management, knowledge base, and customer interactions.

Key Features:

- **Case Management:** This is the backbone of Service Cloud. It allows you to track customer issues, inquiries, or requests from creation to resolution.
- **Knowledge Base:** A centralized repository of information that can be accessed by both customers and agents to resolve issues quickly.
- **Customer Portal:** A self-service platform where customers can find answers, submit cases, and track their status.
- **Live Chat:** Enables real-time interaction with customers.
- **Email Integration:** Manages customer emails within Salesforce.
- **Field Service:** For businesses that provide on-site service, Service Cloud offers tools to manage field service operations.

CASE MANAGEMENT AND ESCALATION

Effective case management is crucial for customer satisfaction.

Case Creation:

- Cases can be created manually or through various channels like email, phone, or web forms.
- Key information such as customer details, case description, and priority should be captured.

Case Assignment:

- Cases can be assigned to specific agents or queues based on skills, availability, or case type.
- Automatic routing rules can be set up for efficient case distribution.

Case Status:

- Different case statuses (open, in progress, closed, escalated) help track case progress.
- Customizable status definitions can be created to fit specific business needs.

Case Escalation:

- Cases can be escalated to higher-level support teams or managers if necessary.
- Automation can be used to trigger escalation based on case age, priority, or other criteria.

Case Closure:

- Cases are closed when resolved, with the option to reopen if necessary.
- Customer satisfaction surveys can be sent upon case closure.

KNOWLEDGE BASE MANAGEMENT

A well-organized knowledge base empowers both customers and agents.

Article Creation:

- Create articles covering common issues, solutions, and product information.
- Use a clear and concise writing style.
- Include relevant keywords and tags for easy search.

Article Organization:

- Categorize articles into folders or categories for better navigation.
- Utilize a hierarchical structure for efficient organization.

Search Functionality:

- Implement a robust search function to help users find relevant information quickly.
- Consider using natural language search for improved results.

Article Publishing:

- Make articles accessible to both customers and agents through the customer portal and agent console.
- Regularly review and update articles to ensure accuracy and relevance.

CUSTOMER SERVICE AUTOMATION (MACROS, AUTO-RESPONSE)

Automation can significantly improve agent productivity and customer satisfaction.

Macros:

- Predefined sets of actions that can be executed with a single click.
- Create macros for common tasks like case updates, email replies, or knowledge base searches.
- Improve agent efficiency and consistency.

Auto-Response:

- Automatically send pre-written messages based on case creation or updates.
- Acknowledge case receipt and provide estimated response times.
- Offer self-service options or direct customers to the knowledge base.

FIELD SERVICE MANAGEMENT

For businesses that provide on-site service, Service Cloud offers tools to optimize field operations.

Key Features:

- **Dispatch:** Assign service appointments to technicians based on skills, location, and availability.
- **Mobile App:** Equip technicians with mobile access to case information, inventory, and customer data.
- **Scheduling:** Optimize appointment scheduling to improve efficiency and customer satisfaction.
- **Parts Management:** Track inventory and manage parts usage.
- **Mobile Payments:** Enable on-site payments.

COLLABORATION AND PRODUCTIVITY

Effective collaboration is essential for delivering excellent customer service.

Chatter Basics and Collaboration Features

Chatter is Salesforce's social collaboration platform.

- **Internal Communication:** Share information, ask questions, and collaborate with colleagues.
- **Groups:** Create groups for specific teams or projects.
- **Files:** Share files and documents within Chatter.
- **Feed:** Stay updated on activities and discussions.

Files and Content Management

Efficiently manage files and documents within Salesforce.

- **Content Library:** Store and organize files and documents.
- **Version Control:** Track changes to files over time.
- **Document Sharing:** Control access to files based on user permissions.
- **Integration with Other Systems:** Integrate with external file storage systems.

Mobile Access and Salesforce Mobile App

Empower your team with mobile access to Salesforce.

- **Salesforce Mobile App:** Provides access to core Salesforce features on mobile devices.
- **Offline Capabilities:** Work offline and sync data when connected.
- **Custom Mobile Apps:** Build custom mobile apps for specific needs.
- **Mobile Optimization:** Ensure optimal performance on different devices.

Email Integration and Lightning Sync

Seamlessly integrate email with Salesforce.

- **Email-to-Case:** Convert incoming emails into cases.
- **Email Templates:** Create email templates for common responses.

- **Email Logging:** Track email activity related to cases and contacts.
- **Lightning Sync:** Synchronize contacts, events, and tasks between Salesforce and email.

Productivity Tools (Tasks, Events, Calendar)

Improve time management and organization.

- **Tasks:** Create, assign, and track tasks.
- **Events:** Schedule appointments and meetings.
- **Calendar:** View and manage schedules.
- **Reminders:** Set reminders for tasks and events.
- **Integration with Outlook:** Synchronize calendars and contacts.

By leveraging these Service Cloud features, businesses can enhance customer satisfaction, improve agent productivity, and streamline support operations.

REPORTING AND ANALYTICS

Reports and dashboards are the cornerstone of data-driven decision making in Salesforce. They provide insights into your business performance and help you identify trends, opportunities, and areas for improvement.

Reports:
- **Purpose:** To extract specific data from your Salesforce org and present it in a tabular format.
- **Types:** Summary reports, tabular reports, matrix reports, and joined reports.
- **Creation:** Use the Report Builder to create reports based on objects and fields.
- **Filters:** Apply filters to refine the data displayed in the report.
- **Grouping:** Group data by specific fields to summarize information.
- **Sorting:** Arrange data in ascending or descending order.

Dashboards:
- **Purpose:** To visually represent key performance indicators (KPIs) and trends.
- **Components:** Dashboards are composed of report charts, metrics, and visual force components.
- **Creation:** Use the Dashboard Builder to create dashboards.
- **Layout:** Arrange components on the dashboard to tell a story.
- **Sharing:** Share dashboards with specific users or groups.

UNDERSTANDING REPORT TYPES AND FILTERS

To create effective reports, you need to understand the different report types and how to use filters effectively.

Report Types:
- **Summary Reports:** Provide aggregated data, such as totals, averages, and counts.

- **Tabular Reports:** Display detailed data in a tabular format.
- **Matrix Reports:** Combine summary and tabular reports for cross-tabulated data.
- **Joined Reports:** Combine data from multiple related objects.
  Filters:
- **Purpose:** To refine the data displayed in a report.
- **Types:** Basic filters, summary filters, and cross filters.
- **Criteria:** Use operators like equals, greater than, less than, and contains to filter data.
- **Multiple Filters:** Combine multiple filters to create complex criteria.

DATA VISUALIZATION AND STORYTELLING

Effective data visualization transforms data into insights that can be easily understood.

- **Chart Types:** Use appropriate chart types to represent different types of data (bar charts, line charts, pie charts, etc.).
- **Color and Formatting:** Use colors and formatting to enhance visual appeal and clarity.
- **Storytelling:** Create a narrative with your data by highlighting key trends and insights.
- **Annotations:** Add annotations to explain data points or provide context.

SHARING REPORTS AND DASHBOARDS

Sharing reports and dashboards is crucial for collaboration and decision-making.

- **Public Reports and Dashboards:** Make reports and dashboards accessible to all users.
- **Private Reports and Dashboards:** Restrict access to specific users or groups.
- **Report Subscriptions:** Schedule email delivery of reports.
- **Dashboard Subscriptions:** Subscribe users to dashboard updates.

Salesforce Analytics Cloud (Basic Overview)

Salesforce Analytics Cloud (previously known as Einstein Analytics) provides advanced analytics capabilities.

- **Data Discovery:** Explore data interactively to uncover insights.
- **Predictive Analytics:** Build predictive models to forecast future trends.
- **Data Visualization:** Create stunning visualizations with interactive dashboards.
- **Collaboration:** Share insights with teams and stakeholders.

AUTOMATION AND WORKFLOW

Automation can significantly improve efficiency and productivity.

Creating and Managing Workflow Rules

Workflow rules automate actions based on specific record changes.
- **Criteria:** Define conditions that trigger the workflow.
- **Actions:** Specify actions to be performed, such as sending email alerts, updating fields, or creating tasks.
- **Evaluation Criteria:** Determine when to evaluate the rule (created, every time it's edited, or when a field changes).
- **Rule Order:** Define the order in which multiple workflow rules are evaluated.

Process Builder and Automation

Process Builder offers a more visual and intuitive way to create automated processes.
- **Processes:** Create complex automation workflows with multiple steps.
- **Immediate Actions:** Execute actions immediately when a record is created or updated.
- **Time-Based Actions:** Schedule actions to occur at a specific time or interval.

- **Criteria-Based Actions:** Execute actions based on specific conditions.

Approval Processes

Route records through an approval process for review and sign-off.

- **Approval Steps:** Define multiple approval steps with different approvers.
- **Approval Actions:** Specify actions to be taken after approval or rejection.
- **Escalation Rules:** Define what happens if an approval is not completed within a specified time.

Validation Rules and Formulas

Ensure data accuracy and consistency with validation rules and formulas.
- **Validation Rules:** Prevent invalid data from being entered.
- **Error Messages:** Provide clear error messages to guide users.
- **Formula Fields:** Calculate values based on other fields.
- **Summary Formulas:** Calculate summary values for reports.

Email Alerts and Notifications

Keep users informed with timely email alerts and notifications.

- **Email Alerts:** Send email notifications based on specific events.
- **Notification User Interface:** Display notifications within the Salesforce interface.
- **Push Notifications:** Deliver notifications to mobile devices.

By effectively utilizing reporting, analytics, and automation, you can optimize business processes, improve decision-making, and enhance overall Salesforce performance.

APPEXCHANGE AND CUSTOMIZATION

AppExchange is Salesforce's online marketplace where you can find thousands of pre-built apps to extend the functionality of your Salesforce org. These apps cover a wide range of business needs, from sales and marketing to customer service and HR.

How AppExchange Works:

- **Search and Discovery:** You can search for apps based on specific keywords, categories, or industry.
- **App Details:** Each app listing provides information about its features, pricing, customer reviews, and support.
- **Free Trials:** Many apps offer free trials to allow you to test them before purchasing.
- **Installation:** Once you've selected an app, you can install it directly into your Salesforce org.

Types of Apps:

- **Enterprise Apps:** These are large-scale applications that address complex business needs.
- **Component Apps:** Smaller, focused apps that provide specific functionalities.
- **Data Apps:** Apps that integrate with external data sources.
- **Mobile Apps:** Apps designed for use on mobile devices.

Key Considerations for App Installation:

- **Compatibility:** Ensure the app is compatible with your Salesforce edition and other installed apps.
- **Data Security:** Review the app's data security practices and permissions.
- **Cost:** Understand the pricing model (one-time purchase, subscription, usage-based).
- **Support:** Evaluate the app provider's support options.

- **Customization:** Consider if the app can be customized to meet your specific requirements.

CUSTOMIZING THE SALESFORCE USER INTERFACE

While AppExchange offers many pre-built solutions, you may need to customize the Salesforce user interface to align with your business processes and user preferences.

Customization Options:
- **Page Layouts:** Modify the layout of record detail pages to display the most relevant information.
- **Tabs:** Control which objects and custom applications appear in the navigation bar.
- **Lightning App Builder:** Create custom Lightning apps with a drag-and-drop interface.
- **Visual force Pages:** Develop custom user interfaces using HTML, CSS, and Apex.

Best Practices for Customization:
- **User-Centric Design:** Focus on user needs and preferences.
- **Consistency:** Maintain a consistent look and feel throughout the interface.
- **Performance Optimization:** Ensure the customized interface loads quickly.
- **Testing:** Thoroughly test customizations before deploying to production.

LIGHTNING APP BUILDER BASICS

Lightning App Builder is a powerful tool for creating custom user experiences without coding.

Key Features:
- **Drag-and-Drop Interface:** Easily assemble components to build pages and apps.

- **Prebuilt Components:** Utilize standard components like record pages, lists, and charts.
- **Custom Components:** Create custom components for specific needs.
- **Responsiveness:** Build apps that adapt to different screen sizes.
  Creating Lightning Apps:
- **Define App:** Specify the name, label, and icon for the app.
- **Add Pages:** Create different pages within the app with specific layouts.
- **Configure Components:** Add and configure components on each page.
- **Navigation:** Define the navigation structure for the app.

BUILDING CUSTOM VISUAL FORCE PAGES

For more complex customizations, Visual force allows you to create custom user interfaces using HTML, CSS, and Apex.

Key Components:

- **Pages:** Create custom pages with specific layouts and content.
- **Controllers:** Write Apex code to handle page logic and data.
- **Components:** Build reusable UI components.
- **Standard Controllers:** Access standard Salesforce objects and data.
  Best Practices for Visual force:
- **Follow Salesforce Standards:** Adhere to Salesforce UI guidelines.
- **Optimize Performance:** Write efficient Visual force code.
- **Security:** Protect against vulnerabilities like cross-site scripting (XSS) and SQL injection.
- **Testing:** Thoroughly test Visual force pages to ensure correct functionality.

Developing Custom Apex Code

Apex is Salesforce's proprietary programming language that allows you to extend platform functionality.

Key Uses:

- **Triggers:** Execute code automatically when records are created, updated, or deleted.
- **Controllers:** Handle logic for Visual force pages.
- **Batch Apex:** Process large volumes of data efficiently.
- **Scheduled Jobs:** Run code at specific intervals.

Apex Basics:
- **Data Types:** Understand basic data types like String, Integer, Date, and SObject.
- **SOQL:** Query data from Salesforce objects.
- **DML Operations:** Create, update, and delete records.
- **Governor Limits:** Be aware of Apex execution limits.

Best Practices for Apex Development:
- **Write Clean and Maintainable Code:** Use meaningful variable names, comments, and code formatting.
- **Test Thoroughly:** Write unit tests to ensure code quality.
- **Optimize Performance:** Avoid unnecessary database queries and bulkify code.
- **Security:** Protect against vulnerabilities like SQL injection and data leakage.

By effectively combining AppExchange apps, custom development, and Salesforce's built-in tools, you can create a tailored Salesforce environment that meets your organization's unique needs.

QUESTIONS

1. Which of the following settings cannot be modified directly from the Company Information page?

    A) Company Address

    B) Primary Contact

    C) Default Locale

    D) Fiscal Year

2. What is the maximum number of custom profiles that can be created in Salesforce?

    A) 500

    B) 1000

    C) Unlimited

    D) 2000

3. How can the fiscal year settings in Salesforce be defined?

    A) Calendar Year

    B) Custom Fiscal Year

    C) Standard Fiscal Year

    D) All of the above

4. Which of the following can be set up through Company Settings?

    A) Business Hours

    B) Login IP Ranges

    C) Password Policies

    D) Custom Fields

5. What happens if the "Grant Access Using Hierarchies" option is disabled for a custom object?

    A) Users can still view records they own

    B) Sharing rules override the option

C) Only system administrators can access the records

D) The object records cannot be shared via role hierarchy

6. Which of the following profiles can be assigned to users?

A) System Administrator

B) Standard User

C) Read Only

D) All of the above

7. What feature allows an administrator to log in as another user?

A) Login IP Restrictions

B) Permission Sets

C) Login Access Policies

D) Grant Login Access

8. Which permission is needed to deactivate a user?

A) Modify All Data

B) View All Data

C) Manage Users

D) System Administrator

9. When assigning a new user license, which license type allows for the creation of up to 2,000 custom objects?

A) Salesforce

B) Salesforce Platform

C) Salesforce Identity

D) Salesforce Chatter

10. Which of the following fields is not mandatory when creating a new user in Salesforce?

A) Username

B) Email

C) Role

D) Alias

11. What is the purpose of the "My Domain" feature in Salesforce?

A) Customizes the Salesforce URL

B) Enhances security with domain specific login

C) Allows branding with custom logo and colors

D) All of the above

12. Which of the following statements about Profiles and Permission Sets is true?

A) Profiles control what users can do, while Permission Sets grant additional permissions

B) Permission Sets control what users can do, while Profiles grant additional permissions

C) Both are used to restrict access

D) Profiles and Permission Sets cannot be used together

13. What does the Role Hierarchy control in Salesforce?

A) Object permissions

B) Record level access

C) Field level security

D) App access

14. Which feature allows users to view records they don't own based on criteria defined by an administrator?

A) Sharing Rules

B) Role Hierarchy

C) Organization Wide Defaults

D) Permission Sets

15. In Salesforce, which of the following is not a standard profile?

A) Standard User

B) Contract Manager

C) Marketing User

D) Finance User

16. Which standard object is used to manage potential revenue from sales?

A) Lead

B) Opportunity

C) Account

D) Contact

17. What is the limit for the number of custom fields that can be created per object in Salesforce?

A) 500

B) 800

C) 1000

D) 200

18. Which of the following can be used to create a many to many relationship between two objects?

A) Lookup Relationship

B) Master Detail Relationship

C) Junction Object

D) Hierarchical Relationship

19. Which type of field cannot be made a unique field in Salesforce?

A) Text

B) Email

C) Number

D) Long Text Area

20. What is the use of the Schema Builder in Salesforce?

A) Import Data

41

B) Build Reports

C) View and modify data model

D) Deploy Apps

21. Which standard object is used to capture information about an individual or organization that is not yet a customer?

A) Lead

B) Account

C) Opportunity

D) Contact

22. What feature can be used to automate lead assignment in Salesforce?

A) Lead Assignment Rules

B) Lead Queues

C) Lead Workflow Rules

D) Lead Scoring

23. In Salesforce, what is the maximum number of leads that can be captured through Web to Lead per day?

A) 500

B) 1000

C) 2000

D) 5000

24. What is the purpose of Campaign Influence in Salesforce?

A) Track email campaigns

B) Track sales performance

C) Attribute revenue to marketing campaigns

D) Manage campaign members

25. Which of the following fields is required when converting a lead?

A) Company

B) Email

C) Status

D) Phone

26. Which object is primarily used to track customer support issues in Salesforce?

A) Case

B) Opportunity

C) Lead

D) Solution

27. What feature allows users to search and browse articles in Salesforce?

A) Knowledge Base

B) Solution Manager

C) Article Management

D) Content Library

28. What is the purpose of Case Assignment Rules in Salesforce?

A) Automatically assign cases to users or queues based on criteria

B) Track case resolution time

C) Escalate cases

D) Merge duplicate cases

29. Which of the following is not a component of the Service Cloud Console?

A) List View

B) Interaction Log

C) Utility Bar

D) Dashboard

30. How can you ensure that a case is escalated if not resolved within a specified time?

A) Case Assignment Rules

B) Escalation Rules

C) Auto Response Rules

D) Validation Rules

31. Which of the following is not a standard Salesforce activity type?

    A) Task

    B) Event

    C) Call

    D) Note

32. What does the "Follow" button on a record allow a user to do?

    A) Receive updates about the record in their Chatter feed

    B) Edit the record

    C) Delete the record

    D) Share the record with other users

33. Which feature in Salesforce allows users to collaborate on records?

    A) Chatter

    B) Groups

    C) Teams

    D) Feed Tracking

34. What is the purpose of the Salesforce Calendar?

    A) Track Opportunities

    B) Schedule Events and Tasks

    C) Manage Leads

    D) Monitor Campaigns

35. Which activity feature allows you to relate multiple contacts to an event or task?

    A) Event Relations

    B) Activity Linking

C) Shared Activities

D) Task Linking

36. What is the maximum file size for files uploaded to Salesforce?

A) 2GB

B) 5MB

C) 10MB

D) 25MB

37. What is the purpose of the Data Import Wizard in Salesforce?

A) Export Data

B) Import data from external sources

C) Sync data with other systems

D) Delete records

38. Which tool can be used to schedule regular data backups in Salesforce?

A) Data Loader

B) Data Export

C) Data Import Wizard

D) Data Integrator

39. Which feature allows users to find and merge duplicate records?

A) Duplicate Management

B) Data Cleansing

C) Data Quality

D) Duplicate Rules

40. What is the maximum number of records that can be imported using the Data Import Wizard at one time?

A) 10,000

B) 20,000

C) 50,000

D) 100,000

41. What is a Report Type in Salesforce?

    A) A template for creating reports

    B) A way to schedule reports

    C) A filter for report data

    D) A report sharing setting

42. Which feature allows users to visualize data in a graphical format in Salesforce?

    A) Dashboards

    B) Reports

    C) Charts

    D) Analytics

43. What is the maximum number of reports that can be added to a dashboard?

    A) 5

    B) 10

    C) 20

    D) 50

44. How can you share a report with other users in Salesforce?

    A) Report Sharing Settings

    B) Folder Sharing

    C) Report Link

    D) All of the above

45. Which of the following is not a type of chart available in Salesforce reports?

    A) Line Chart

    B) Bar Chart

    C) Histogram

    D) Funnel Chart

46. What is a Workflow Rule in Salesforce?

   A) A tool to import data

   B) A feature to automate business processes

   C) A report customization tool

   D) A way to manage user permissions

47. Which component is not part of a Workflow Rule?

   A) Criteria

   B) Actions

   C) Time Triggers

   D) Validation Rules

48. What type of action can be performed by a Workflow Rule?

   A) Create Task

   B) Send Email Alert

   C) Update Field

   D) All of the above

49. What is the purpose of a Process Builder in Salesforce?

   A) Import data

   B) Create records

   C) Automate complex business processes

   D) Manage profiles

50. Which feature in Salesforce allows for multistep approval processes?

   A) Workflow Rules

   B) Approval Processes

   C) Validation Rules

   D) Process Builder

51. Which of the following is true about Salesforce1 mobile app?

A) It provides offline access to data

B) It allows access to custom objects

C) It supports mobile only features

D) All of the above

52. What is the purpose of the Mobile Publisher feature in Salesforce?

A) Build custom mobile apps

B) Create mobile responsive pages

C) Publish mobile content

D) Manage mobile notifications

53. Which field cannot be customized for the Salesforce mobile app?

A) Compact Layout

B) Record Pages

C) List Views

D) Search Layout

54. What is the function of Mobile Smart Actions in Salesforce?

A) Automate mobile data entry

B) Enable voice commands

C) Perform quick actions on mobile

D) Sync mobile data

55. Which feature in Salesforce allows for push notifications to mobile devices?

A) Chatter

B) Mobile Alerts

C) Salesforce1 Notifications

D) Workflow Alerts

56. What is AppExchange in Salesforce?

A) A marketplace for Salesforce apps

B) A tool for data integration

C) A community forum

D) A reporting tool

57. Which of the following is not a type of component available on AppExchange?

A) Apps

B) Components

C) Solutions

D) Scripts

58. How can users install an app from AppExchange?

A) Using the Data Import Wizard

B) By downloading and manually uploading

C) Directly from the AppExchange interface

D) Via a third party service

59. Which of the following is a benefit of using AppExchange solutions?

A) Prebuilt functionalities

B) Reduced development time

C) Access to a wider range of tools

D) All of the above

60. What is a "Managed Package" in Salesforce?

A) A collection of prebuilt functionalities

B) A set of API integrations

C) A type of app that can be updated by the provider

D) A bundle of reports and dashboards

61. Which of the following is true about the Service Cloud Console?

A) It provides a unified view of customer interactions

B) It is used to manage marketing campaigns

C) It allows for direct integration with financial software

D) It is used to develop custom apps

62. What is the purpose of the Knowledge object in Salesforce?

    A) Store and manage customer cases

    B) Store and share articles and FAQs

    C) Track sales opportunities

    D) Manage service contracts

63. Which feature is used to automate the routing of cases to the right agents in Salesforce?

    A) Case Assignment Rules

    B) Case Auto Response Rules

    C) Escalation Rules

    D) Case Queues

64. What is a Case Feed in Salesforce?

    A) A log of all changes made to a case

    B) A timeline of case activities

    C) A detailed report of case metrics

    D) A collaborative tool for managing cases

65. What is the purpose of Milestones in Salesforce?

    A) Track key stages in a case resolution process

    B) Manage marketing campaign timelines

    C) Monitor sales pipeline stages

    D) Schedule data backup operations

66. Which Salesforce feature allows users to schedule and manage tasks and events?

    A) Activity Timeline

B) Calendar

C) Task Manager

D) Event Scheduler

67. What is the primary use of Chatter in Salesforce?

A) Real time collaboration and information sharing

B) Task management

C) Case resolution

D) Data backup

68. How can users follow records to receive updates in their Chatter feed?

A) By liking the record

B) By commenting on the record

C) By clicking the Follow button

D) By sharing the record

69. What is the purpose of Chatter Groups?

A) Organize users into collaborative groups

B) Manage user permissions

C) Schedule tasks and events

D) Track sales opportunities

70. Which feature in Salesforce allows users to send direct messages to other users?

A) Chatter Direct

B) Chatter Messenger

C) Chatter Connect

D) Chatter Private

71. What is the primary purpose of the Data Loader in Salesforce?

A) Import large volumes of data

B) Export data to external systems

C) Perform bulk data updates

D) All of the above

72. Which tool can be used to create data backup files in Salesforce?

A) Data Export Service

B) Data Import Wizard

C) Schema Builder

D) Report Builder

73. What is a Matching Rule in Salesforce?

A) A rule to identify duplicate records

B) A rule to merge duplicate records

C) A rule to update records

D) A rule to import records

74. Which of the following cannot be managed using the Data Import Wizard?

A) Accounts

B) Contacts

C) Leads

D) Opportunities

75. Which feature in Salesforce helps to maintain data quality by preventing the creation of duplicate records?

A) Validation Rules

B) Duplicate Rules

C) Workflow Rules

D) Escalation Rules

76. What is the purpose of a Custom Report Type in Salesforce?

A) Customize the layout of a report

B) Define the objects and fields available for reporting

C) Set report filters

D) Share reports with users

77. Which feature allows users to filter report data dynamically in Salesforce?

A) Custom Report Types

B) Report Filters

C) Dynamic Dashboards

D) Report Snapshots

78. What is a Summary Report in Salesforce?

A) A report that groups data and provides subtotals

B) A report that provides a flat list of records

C) A report that tracks trends over time

D) A report that shows data in a matrix format

79. Which component is not part of a Salesforce Dashboard?

A) Report

B) Gauge

C) Chart

D) Field

80. How can users ensure that their reports always reflect the most recent data?

A) By refreshing the report manually

B) By scheduling the report to run at specific intervals

C) By using real time data integration

D) All of the above

81. Which Salesforce feature allows you to automate repetitive business processes?

A) Workflow Rules

B) Process Builder

C) Approval Processes

D) All of the above

82. What is the maximum number of time triggers allowed in a single Workflow Rule?

A) 5

B) 10

C) 20

D) 50

83. What type of field update action can be performed by a Workflow Rule?

A) Update the value of a field

B) Create a new record

C) Delete a record

D) Export data

84. Which feature in Salesforce allows you to send email alerts based on specific criteria?

A) Email Templates

B) Workflow Rules

C) Auto Response Rules

D) Escalation Rules

85. What is the purpose of an Approval Process in Salesforce?

A) Automate approval of records based on criteria

B) Schedule data backups

C) Manage user permissions

D) Track sales performance

86. Which feature in Salesforce allows for customizing the Salesforce mobile app?

A) Mobile Layouts

B) Mobile Publisher

C) Mobile Smart Actions

D) Mobile Alerts

87. What is the primary use of the Salesforce mobile app?

   A) Access Salesforce data on mobile devices

   B) Schedule data backups

   C) Manage user permissions

   D) Track sales performance

88. Which field can be customized for the Salesforce mobile app to enhance the user experience?

   A) Compact Layouts

   B) List Views

   C) Search Layouts

   D) All of the above

89. What is the purpose of the Mobile Navigation Menu in Salesforce?

   A) Provide access to commonly used features

   B) Customize mobile app appearance

   C) Schedule mobile notifications

   D) Manage mobile data sync

90. How can users receive notifications on their mobile devices for updates in Salesforce?

   A) By configuring Mobile Alerts

   B) By setting up Chatter Notifications

   C) By enabling Salesforce1 Notifications

   D) All of the above

91. Which of the following best describes an AppExchange solution?

   A) A prebuilt app or component for Salesforce

   B) A tool for data integration

   C) A reporting tool

D) A data backup service

92. How can an administrator manage installed packages from AppExchange?

    A) Using the Installed Packages page

    B) Through the AppExchange website

    C) By contacting Salesforce support

    D) Using the Data Import Wizard

93. Which type of AppExchange solution cannot be modified by the installing organization?

    A) Managed Packages

    B) Unmanaged Packages

    C) Custom Apps

    D) Visual force Pages

94. What is the purpose of AppExchange partners in the Salesforce ecosystem?

    A) Provide support and services

    B) Develop and distribute apps

    C) Offer training and consulting

    D) All of the above

95. Which of the following is a best practice for evaluating AppExchange solutions before installation?

    A) Reading reviews and ratings

    B) Checking for certifications

    C) Testing in a sandbox environment

    D) All of the above

96. Which feature allows users to track the progress of service level agreements (SLAs) in Salesforce?

    A) Milestones

    B) Entitlements

C) Case Escalations

D) Service Contracts

97. What is the function of the Case Team feature in Salesforce?

A) Assign multiple users to a case

B) Track case metrics

C) Automate case routing

D) Merge duplicate cases

98. Which of the following can be created and managed using the Service Console in Salesforce?

A) Cases

B) Opportunities

C) Leads

D) Campaigns

99. How can knowledge articles be organized in Salesforce Knowledge?

A) By Categories

B) By Data Type

C) By User Role

D) By Custom Fields

100. Which feature in Salesforce allows customers to find answers to their questions on their own?

A) Self Service Portal

B) Knowledge Base

C) Case Management

D) Chatter

101. Which Salesforce feature allows users to assign tasks to other users?

A) Activity Timeline

B) Task Manager

C) Calendar

D) Chatter

102. What is the purpose of the Activity Timeline in Salesforce?

A) Provide a historical view of activities related to a record

B) Schedule future tasks and events

C) Track sales opportunities

D) Manage user permissions

103. How can users ensure they do not miss important updates in their Chatter feed?

A) By setting up email notifications

B) By following relevant records and groups

C) By creating custom feeds

D) All of the above

104. What is a Chatter Poll in Salesforce?

A) A feature to survey opinions

B) A tool to assign tasks

C) A way to schedule events

D) A data backup service

105. Which feature in Salesforce allows users to create, share, and collaborate on documents?

A) Chatter Files

B) Document Manager

C) File Sharing

D) Content Library

106. Which tool can be used to prevent duplicate records in Salesforce?

A) Validation Rules

B) Duplicate Rules

C) Workflow Rules

D) Escalation Rules

107. What is a Custom Report Type in Salesforce?

    A) A report format that can be customized

    B) A way to define the relationships and fields available for reporting

    C) A data export tool

    D) A data import tool

108. How can users automate the deletion of obsolete data in Salesforce?

    A) Using Data Export Service

    B) Using Data Loader

    C) Using Mass Delete Records

    D) Using Workflow Rules

109. Which feature in Salesforce helps maintain data quality by identifying and merging duplicate records?

    A) Data Cleansing

    B) Duplicate Management

    C) Data Quality Rules

    D) Data Merging

110. What is the maximum number of records that can be exported using the Data Export Service in Salesforce?

    A) 50,000

    B) 100,000

    C) 500,000

    D) No limit

111. Which feature allows users to display multiple reports on a single page in Salesforce?

    A) Report Snapshots

B) Dynamic Dashboards

C) Report Charts

D) Dashboard Components

112. What is the purpose of Conditional Highlighting in Salesforce reports?

A) Highlight cells based on criteria

B) Schedule report refreshes

C) Customize report filters

D) Share reports with other users

113. Which type of report in Salesforce provides a visual representation of trends over time?

A) Summary Report

B) Tabular Report

C) Matrix Report

D) Analytical Snapshot

114. What is the purpose of a Bucket Field in Salesforce reports?

A) Categorize report records without creating a formula or custom field

B) Aggregate data from multiple fields

C) Create cross object summaries

D) Set up report filters

115. How can users ensure that sensitive data is not included in shared reports?

A) Using Field Level Security

B) By creating private reports

C) By applying report filters

D) By using report folders

116. Which Salesforce feature allows you to define a series of steps for record approvals?

A) Workflow Rules

B) Approval Processes

C) Process Builder

D) Validation Rules

117. What is a Time Dependent Workflow Action in Salesforce?

A) An action that is triggered at a specific time

B) An action that is triggered based on a field value

C) An action that runs in real time

D) An action that is scheduled to run periodically

118. Which feature allows users to automate complex business processes using a visual interface?

A) Workflow Rules

B) Process Builder

C) Approval Processes

D) Validation Rules

119. What is the maximum number of actions that can be performed by a single Workflow Rule?

A) 5

B) 10

C) 20

D) Unlimited

120. How can users ensure that records are updated automatically based on certain criteria in Salesforce?

A) Using Validation Rules

B) Using Workflow Rules

C) Using Approval Processes

D) Using Process Builder

121. What is the purpose of the Mobile Publisher feature in Salesforce?

A) Customize the mobile app interface

B) Publish custom mobile apps

C) Schedule mobile notifications

D) Sync mobile data with Salesforce

122. Which feature in Salesforce allows for push notifications to mobile devices?

A) Mobile Alerts

B) Salesforce1 Notifications

C) Chatter Notifications

D) Workflow Alerts

123. Which layout can be customized specifically for mobile devices in Salesforce?

A) Compact Layout

B) Page Layout

C) Mobile Layout

D) Record Layout

124. How can users access Salesforce data on their mobile devices?

A) By using the Salesforce mobile app

B) By using a web browser

C) By using a mobile emulator

D) By using a desktop sync tool

125. What is the purpose of the Mobile Smart Actions feature in Salesforce?

A) Automate repetitive tasks on mobile devices

B) Enable voice commands

C) Provide quick actions for common tasks

D) Sync data between mobile and desktop

126. Which of the following best describes a Managed Package on AppExchange?

A) An app that can be updated by the provider

B) An app that cannot be modified by the user

C) An app that includes prebuilt components

D) An app that integrates with external systems

127. How can users find solutions to specific business problems on AppExchange?

A) By browsing categories

B) By using the search feature

C) By reading reviews and ratings

D) All of the above

128. Which feature in Salesforce allows users to extend the functionality of their org with third party apps?

A) AppExchange

B) Data Loader

C) Workflow Rules

D) Custom Objects

129. What is a key benefit of using AppExchange solutions in Salesforce?

A) Reduced development time

B) Access to a wider range of tools

C) Prebuilt functionalities

D) All of the above

130. How can users evaluate the reliability of an AppExchange solution before installation?

A) By reading customer reviews

B) By checking provider certifications

C) By testing in a sandbox environment

D) All of the above

131. What is the function of the Entitlements feature in Salesforce?

    A) Track service level agreements (SLAs)

    B) Manage customer accounts

    C) Automate case routing

    D) Provide knowledge articles

132. How can users ensure that cases are resolved within a specific timeframe?

    A) Using Escalation Rules

    B) Using Case Assignment Rules

    C) Using Entitlements and Milestones

    D) Using Workflow Rules

133. Which feature allows users to create and share knowledge articles in Salesforce?

    A) Knowledge Base

    B) Content Library

    C) Document Manager

    D) Chatter Files

134. What is the purpose of a Service Contract in Salesforce?

    A) Define the terms of service for customers

    B) Manage customer accounts

    C) Track sales opportunities

    D) Schedule data backups

135. Which feature in Salesforce allows for the automation of responses to customer inquiries?

    A) Auto Response Rules

    B) Workflow Rules

    C) Approval Processes

D) Process Builder

136. Which Salesforce feature allows users to collaborate on tasks and projects?

A) Chatter

B) Activity Timeline

C) Calendar

D) Task Manager

137. What is the purpose of the Chatter Feed in Salesforce?

A) Provide a real time collaboration space

B) Track sales performance

C) Schedule tasks and events

D) Manage user permissions

138. How can users ensure they receive important updates in their Chatter feed?

A) By setting up email notifications

B) By following relevant records and groups

C) By customizing their feed preferences

D) All of the above

139. Which feature in Salesforce allows users to create and manage tasks?

A) Task Manager

B) Activity Timeline

C) Calendar

D) Chatter

140. What is the purpose of the Activity Timeline in Salesforce?

A) Provide a historical view of activities related to a record

B) Schedule future tasks and events

C) Track sales opportunities

D) Manage user permissions

141. What is the purpose of the Data Loader tool in Salesforce?

    A) Import large volumes of data

    B) Export data to external systems

    C) Perform bulk data updates

    D) All of the above

142. How can users prevent duplicate records in Salesforce?

    A) Using Validation Rules

    B) Using Duplicate Rules

    C) Using Workflow Rules

    D) Using Escalation Rules

143. What is a Matching Rule in Salesforce?

    A) A rule to identify duplicate records

    B) A rule to merge duplicate records

    C) A rule to update records

    D) A rule to import records

144. Which feature in Salesforce helps maintain data quality by identifying and merging duplicate records?

    A) Data Cleansing

    B) Duplicate Management

    C) Data Quality Rules

    D) Data Merging

145. How can users automate the deletion of obsolete data in Salesforce?

    A) Using Data Export Service

    B) Using Data Loader

    C) Using Mass Delete Records

    D) Using Workflow Rules

146. What is the purpose of Conditional Highlighting in Salesforce reports?

A) Highlight cells based on criteria

B) Schedule report refreshes

C) Customize report filters

D) Share reports with other users

147. Which type of report in Salesforce provides a visual representation of trends over time?

A) Summary Report

B) Tabular Report

C) Matrix Report

D) Analytical Snapshot

148. What is the purpose of a Bucket Field in Salesforce reports?

A) Categorize report records without creating a formula or custom field

B) Aggregate data from multiple fields

C) Create cross object summaries

D) Set up report filters

149. How can users ensure that sensitive data is not included in shared reports?

A) Using Field Level Security

B) By creating private reports

C) By applying report filters

D) By using report folders

150. Which feature allows users to display multiple reports on a single page in Salesforce?

A) Report Snapshots

B) Dynamic Dashboards

C) Report Charts

D) Dashboard Components

151. Which permission allows a user to create and manage other users in Salesforce?

   A) View All Users

   B) Modify All Data

   C) Manage Users

   D) Customize Application

152. What is the purpose of the Data Loader tool in Salesforce?

   A) To create custom objects

   B) To import and export data

   C) To create validation rules

   D) To manage user profiles

153. Which feature allows you to create custom fields on standard objects?

   A) Custom Objects

   B) Custom Fields

   C) Page Layouts

   D) Record Types

154. What action can be triggered by a workflow rule?

   A) Sending an email alert

   B) Creating a new record

   C) Updating a field value

   D) All of the above

155. Which type of report displays data in a tabular format with rows and columns?

   A) Summary Report

   B) Matrix Report

   C) Tabular Report

   D) Joined Report

156. What is the purpose of Chatter in Salesforce?

    A) To create custom reports

    B) To collaborate with colleagues

    C) To manage user profiles

    D) To import data

157. Which feature provides a responsive and modern user interface in Salesforce?

    A) Classic Experience

    B) Lightning Experience

    C) Visual force Pages

    D) Apex Triggers

158. What is the AppExchange in Salesforce?

    A) A marketplace for third party apps

    B) A feature to create custom objects

    C) A tool for data migration

    D) A module for user training

159. What is the purpose of a Sales Cloud in Salesforce?

    A) To manage customer service cases

    B) To track sales leads and opportunities

    C) To create custom reports

    D) To manage user profiles

160. Which feature allows agents to handle customer inquiries and cases efficiently?

    A) Knowledge Base

    B) Chatter

    C) Reports and Dashboards

    D) Workflow Rules

161. What is the benefit of creating a community in Salesforce?

    A) To manage user profiles

    B) To collaborate with external users

    C) To create custom objects

    D) To import data

162.Cloud Kicks users are experiencing different options when uploading a custom picklist on the Opportunity object depending on the type of opportunity. Where should an administrator update the picklist options?

    A) Fields and relationships

    B) Related lookup filters

    C) Record Type

    D) Picklist value sets

163. An administrator wants to create a form in Salesforce for users to fill out when they lose a client. Which automation tool supports creating a wizard to accomplish this goal?

    A) Process Builder

    B) Approval Process

    C) Outbound Message

    D) Flow Builder

164. The VP of Sales at Universal Containers wants to prevent sales team members from setting an opportunity close date to a past date. What should an administrator configure to meet this requirement?

    A) Assignment Rule

    B) Validation Rule

    C) Field-Level Security

    D) Approval Process

165. Northern Trail Outfitters wants to track ROI for contacts who are key stakeholders for opportunities. The VP of Sales requested that this information be accessible on the opportunity and available for reporting. Which two options

should the administrator configure to meet these requirements? (Choose 2 answers)

A) Customize Campaign Member Role.

B) Add the Campaign Member related list to the Opportunity page layout.

C) Customize Campaign Role.

D) Customize Opportunity Contact Role.

E) Add the Opportunity Contact Role related list to the Opportunity page layout.

166. Universal Containers aims to enhance the user experience when searching for the correct status on a case. Currently, there is one support process for all case record types with 10 status values. Service reps mention they only need up to five statuses based on the type of case. How should the administrator improve the current implementation?

A) Reduce the number of case status values to five.

B) Create a Screen Flow that shows only the correct values for status and surface the flow in the utility bar of the console.

C) Review which status choices are needed for each record type and create support processes for each that is necessary.

D) Edit the status choices directly on the record type.

167. Northern Trail Outfitters is planning to start generating expense reports in Salesforce that will be sent to an external HR system. The expense reports must be reviewed by both managers and directors before finalization.

Which two tools should an administrator set up to accomplish this task? (Select two.)

A. Quick Action

B. Outbound Message

C. Approval Process

D. Email Alert Action

168. Cloud Kicks is seeking an improved method for tracking its product shipments using Salesforce.

Which field type should an administrator select to record geographic coordinates?

    A. Geolocation

    B. Geofence

    C. Custom Address

    D. External Lookup

169. What are two factors an administrator should consider when managing Salesforce objects? (Select two.)

    A. Custom and standard objects come with predefined fields.

    B. Standard objects are provided by default with Salesforce.

    C. It is possible to create a new standard object.

    D. Master-detail relationships are supported only by standard objects.

170. Users have observed that when they click on a report within a dashboard to view the detailed report, the figures in the report do not match those shown on the dashboard.

What are two possible reasons for this discrepancy? (Select two.)

    A. The report requires refreshing.

    B. The dashboard requires refreshing.

    C. The current user lacks access to the report folder.

    D. There are different permissions for the running dashboard user and the viewer.

171. The marketing team needs to add a new pick list value to the Campaign Member Status field for the upsell promotional campaign.

Which two actions should the administrator take to update the pick list field values? (Select two.)

    A. Add the Campaign Member Statuses related list to the Page Layout.

    B. Edit the picklist values for Campaign Status in Object Manager.

    C. Use mass modification for the Campaign Member Statuses related list.

D. Change the picklist value directly on the Campaign Member Statuses related list.

172. Ursa Solar Major is assessing Salesforce for its service team and wants to identify which standard objects are available by default.

Which three standard objects should an administrator consider for a support use case? (Select three.)

A. Contract

B. Case

C. Ticket

D. Request

E. Account

173. The service manager at Ursa Major Solar wants to notify customers via email and on their website when their cases are received. Different email notifications are needed for medium-priority and high-priority cases compared to low-priority cases. Three email templates have been created for this purpose.

How should an administrator set up this requirement?

A. Create three assignment rules that trigger when cases are created. Add a filter for case priority and select the appropriate email template for each rule.

B. Set up three auto-response rules, configuring one rule entry criterion for each rule and applying a filter based on case priority. Select the corresponding email template for each rule entry.

C. Configure a single workflow rule that triggers when cases are created. Add a filter for case priority and select the appropriate email template for the rule.

D. Create a single auto-response rule with three rule entry criteria and filters for case priority. Choose the appropriate email template for each criterion.

174. The VP of Sales at Dreamhouse Realty wants a dashboard to display enterprise sales data across various teams. The focus is on showing the total sales for the year and how close the total is to the enterprise sales goal.

Which dashboard component will best represent this information as a single value, including the progress towards the goal?

A. Table

B. Stacked Bar

C. Donut

D. Gauge

175. Northern Trail Outfitters has two distinct sales processes: one for business opportunities with four stages and another for partner opportunities with eight stages. Each process requires different page layouts and picklist values.

What should an administrator configure to address these requirements?

A. Validation rules to ensure users provide accurate sales stage information.

B. Separate page layouts to manage picklist values for different opportunity types.

C. Public groups to restrict record types and sales processes for opportunities.

D. Distinct record types and sales processes for each type of opportunity.

176. An administrator has installed a managed package that includes a permission set group with Delete access on several objects. To prevent users in this permission set group from deleting records, what should the administrator do?

A. Use a muting permission set to disable specific permissions within the permission set group.

B. Create a new permission set without Delete access for the relevant objects.

C. Establish a new role to prevent Delete permissions from being inherited by users.

D. Modify the users' profiles to remove Delete access from the objects.

177. Cloud Kicks wants to ensure that users can only select the "Closed Won" stage for Opportunities if a Lead Source has been specified.

How should the administrator achieve this?

A. Set up Lead Source as a dependent picklist for the Opportunity stage field.

B. Configure a validation rule that requires Lead Source to be selected when the stage is set to "Closed Won."

C. Change the Opportunity stage field to read-only on the page layout.

D. Modify the Opportunity stage field to be a dependent picklist based on the Lead Source field.

178. Sales users at Universal Containers are experiencing delays when editing opportunity records, primarily updating the Stage field.

Which two options should the administrator suggest to streamline this process? (Select two.)

A. Add a path for the Stage field to the Opportunity record page.

B. Utilize a Kanban list view for Opportunities.

C. Set up an auto-launched flow to simplify Opportunity editing.

D. Create a simplified Opportunity page layout.

179. An administrator created a record trigger flow to update contacts. How should the administrator reference the values of the active record the flow is running on?

A. Use the {!Contact.Id} global variable.

B. Use the {!Account.Id} record variable.

C. Use the $Record global variable.

D. Use the Get Records element to find the Id.

180. An administrator gets a rush request from Human Resources to remove a user's access to Salesforce Immediately. The user is part of a hierarchy field called Direct Manager.

What should the administrator do to fulfil the request?

A. Freeze the user to prevent them from logging in while removing them from being referenced in the Direct Manager field.

B. Deactivate the user and delete any records where they are referenced in the Direct Manager field.

C. Change the user's profile to read-only while removing them from being referenced in the Direct Manager Field.

D. Delete the user and leave all records where they referenced in the Direct Manager Field without changes.

181. AW Computing (AWC) occasionally works with independent contractors, who the company stores as Contacts in Salesforce. Contractors often change agencies, and AWC wants to maintain the historical accuracy of the record. What should AWC use to track Contacts?

A. Use a partner community to track the Contacts.

B. Create a new Contact record for each agency.

C. Create a Junction object to track many-to-many relationship.

D. Enable Contacts to multiple Accounts.

182. Which two actions should an administrator perform with Case escalation rules? Choose 2 answers

A. Re-open the Case.

B. Send email notifications.

C. Change the Case Priority.

D. Re-assign the Case.

183. The Sales director at Cloud Kicks wants to be able to predict upcoming revenue in the next several fiscal quarters so they can set goals and benchmark how reps are performing.

Which two features should the administrator configure? Choose 2 answers

A. Sales Quotes

B. Opportunity List View

C. Forecasting

D. Opportunity Stages

184. Universal Containers requires a different Lightning page to be displayed when Accounts are viewed in the Sales Console and in the Service Console. How should an administrator meet this requirement?

A. Update page layout assignments.

B. Define multiple record types.

C. Assign Lightning pages as app default.

D. Create different user profiles.

185. Sales reps at Northern Trail Outfitters have asked for a way to change the Probability field value of their Opportunities.

What should an administrator suggest to meet this request?

A. Define a new Stage picklist value.

B. Create a custom field on Opportunity.

C. Configure Forecasting support.

D. Make the field editable on page layouts

186. An administrator at Cloud Kicks is building a flow that needs to search for records that meet certain conditions and store values from those records in variable for use later in the flow.

What flow element should the administrator add?

A. Assignment

B. Get Records

C. Create Records

D. Update Records

187. An administrator at Cloud Kicks has a flow in production that is supposed to create new records.

However, no new records are being created.

What could the issue be?

A. The flow is read only.

B. The flow is inactive.

C. The flow URL is deactivated.

D. The flow trigger is missing.

188. What are three characteristics of a master-detail relationship? Choose 3 answers

A. The master object can be a standard or custom object.

B. Permissions for the detail record are set independently of the master.

C. Each object can have up to five master-detail relationships.

D. Roll-up summaries are supported in master-detail relationships.

E. The owner field on the detail records is the owner of the master record.

189. An administrator at Universal Containers has been asked to prevent users from accessing Salesforce from outside of their network.

What are two considerations for this configuration?

Choose 2 answers

A. IP address restrictions are set on the profile or globally for the org.

B. Users can change their password to avoid login IP restrictions.

C. Enforce Login IP Ranges on Every Request must be selected to enforce IP restrictions.

D. Single sign-on will allow users to log in from anywhere.

190. The administrator at Cloud Kicks has created an approval process for time off requests.

Which two automated actions are available to be added as part of the approval process? Choose 2 answers

A. Field Update

B. Chatter Post

C. Auto launched Flow

D. Email Alert

191. Which two capabilities are considerations when marking a field as required in Object Manager? Choose 2 answers

A. The field is not required to save records via the API on that object.

B. The field is universally required to save a record on that object.

C. The field is added to every page layout on that object.

D. The field is optional when saving records via web-to-lead and web-to-case

192. Which item is available in a Lightning App where visibility is limited to the Salesforce Mobile App?

A. Today

B. Favorites

C. Utility Bar.

D. Home Page.

E. The field is optional when saving records via web-to-lead and web-to-case

193. An administrator has assigned a permission set group with the two-factor authentication for User Interface Logins permissions and the two-factor authentication for API Logins permission to a group of users. Which two prompts will happen when one of the users attempts to log in to Data Loader? Choose 2 answers

A. Users need to connect an authenticator app to their Salesforce account.

B. Users need to get a security token from a trusted network using Reset My Security Token.

C. Users need to download and install an authenticator app on their mobile device.

D. Users need to enter a verification code from email or SMS, whichever has higher priority.

194. A user at Cloud Kicks is having issues logging in to Salesforce. The user asks the administrator to reset their password.

Which two options should the administrator consider when resetting the user's password? Choose 2 answers

A. Resetting the password will change the user's password policy.

B. Single sign-on users can reset their own passwords using the forgot password link.

C. Resetting a locked-out user's password automatically unlocks the user's account.

D. After resetting a password, the user may be required to activate their device to successfully log in to Salesforce.

195. Which two solutions could an administrator find on the AppExchange to enhance their organization?

Choose 2 answers

    A. Communities

    B. Consultants

    C. Components

    D. Customers

196. Sales and Customer Care at Ursa Major Solar need to see different fields on the Case related list from the Account record. Sales users want to see Case created date and status while Customer Care would like to see owner, status, and contact.

What should the administrator use to achieve this?

    A. Related Lookup Filters

    B. Compact Layout Editor

    C. Page Layout editor

    D. Search Layout Editor

197. The support manager at Cloud Kicks wants to respond to customers as quickly as possible. They have requested that the response include the top five troubleshooting tips that could help solve the customer's issue. What should the administrator suggest to meet these requirement?

    A. Auto-Response Rules

    B. Email Alerts

    C. Knowledge Articles

    D. Assignment Rules

198. Northern Trail Outfitters has a custom quick action on Account that creates a new Case.

How should an administrator make the quick action available on the Salesforce mobile app?

A. Create a custom Lightning App with the action.

B. Modify compact Case page layout to include the action.

C. Include the action in the Salesforce Mobile Navigation menu.

D. Add the Salesforce Mobile and Lightning Experience action to the page layout.

199. The administrator at Dream House Realty added an email quick action to the Case page layout and is unable to see the action on the case feed. Which feature must be enabled to ensure the quick action will be displayed as expected?

A. Email Notifications

B. Email-to-Case

C. Email Alerts

D. Email Templates

200. An administrator has reviewed an upcoming critical update. How should the administrator proceed with activation of the critical update?

A. Activate the critical update in a sandbox.

B. Allow the critical update to auto-activate.

C. Activate the critical update in production.

D. Allow the critical update to auto-activate in a sandbox.

201. An Administrator wants to trigger a follow-up task for the opportunity owner when they close an opportunity as won and another task after 60 days to check in with the customer. Which two automation tools should the administrator use? Choose 2 answers

A. process builder

B. workflow Rule

C. Field Update

D. Outbound Message

ANSWERS

1] Answer: D) Fiscal Year

Explanation:

The Company Information page in Salesforce is primarily for managing basic organizational details. It's where you can find and modify core information about your company, such as its address, primary contact, and default locale.

Company Address and Primary Contact are essential pieces of information about your organization and can be easily modified on the Company Information page.

Default Locale defines the language and regional settings for your organization, and it's also configurable on the Company Information page.

However, the Fiscal Year is a more complex setting that involves defining the starting month, whether the year is based on the starting or ending month, and other financial considerations. Due to its complexity and potential impact on various system functionalities, the Fiscal Year setting is managed in a separate section within Salesforce Setup, specifically under Company Information > Financial Information.

Therefore, the Fiscal Year cannot be directly modified from the Company Information page.

Additional Considerations:

Modifying the Fiscal Year can have implications on reporting, forecasting, and other financial processes. It's essential to carefully plan and consider the impact before making changes.

Understanding the difference between the Company Information page and the Financial Information section is crucial for efficient Salesforce administration.

By grasping these concepts, you can effectively manage your organization's settings within Salesforce.

2] Answer: A) 500

Explanation:

Salesforce imposes a limit of 500 custom profiles per user license type. This means that the total number of custom profiles you can create depends on the number of user licenses your organization has purchased.

Professional Edition: There's a further limitation of 3 custom profiles.

Enterprise, Performance, Unlimited, and Developer Editions: Allow for up to 500 custom profiles per user license type.

It's essential to understand this limitation to effectively plan your organization's user roles and permissions.

Why other options are incorrect:

B) 1000, C) Unlimited, and D) 2000: These options exceed the actual limit of 500 custom profiles per user license type.

By understanding the maximum number of custom profiles and the limitations based on your Salesforce edition, you can optimize user management and security within your organization.

3] Answer: D) All of the above

Explanation:

Salesforce offers flexibility in defining your fiscal year to align with your organization's specific needs. Here's a breakdown of the options:

- Calendar Year: This is the most straightforward option, where the fiscal year aligns with the standard Gregorian calendar (January to December).
- Custom Fiscal Year: This allows you to define a fiscal year that starts on any month of the year, with any number of periods (quarters or months) and custom names for those periods. This is ideal for organizations with unique financial cycles.
- Standard Fiscal Year: This option follows the Gregorian calendar but allows you to choose a different start month for your fiscal year. For instance, you can have a fiscal year that starts in April and ends in March.

By providing these options, Salesforce ensures that businesses of all sizes and industries can accurately represent their financial cycles within the platform.

Understanding these options is crucial for financial reporting, forecasting, and budgeting within Salesforce.

4] Answer: B) Login IP Ranges

Explanation:

Company Settings in Salesforce is where you configure the basic settings that apply to your entire organization. This includes security-related settings, such as controlling access to your Salesforce org.

- Login IP Ranges can be set up here to restrict access to your Salesforce org to specific IP addresses, enhancing security.
- Business Hours are defined under the General Settings section, not Company Settings.
- Password Policies are also configured under Security Controls, separate from Company Settings.
- Custom Fields are created at the object level, not within Company Settings.

By understanding where different settings are located, you can efficiently manage your Salesforce organization's configuration.

5]Answer: D) The object records cannot be shared via role hierarchy

Explanation:

The "Grant Access Using Hierarchies" option is crucial for enabling data sharing based on the role hierarchy within Salesforce. When this option is enabled, users higher in the hierarchy can access records owned by users lower in the hierarchy, even if the default sharing setting is private.

If this option is disabled for a custom object, it effectively prevents the use of role hierarchy for sharing records of that object. This means that users will only be able to access records based on their individual permissions and any explicit sharing rules applied to the records.

Why other options are incorrect:

A) Users can still view records they own: This is true regardless of whether the "Grant Access Using Hierarchies" option is enabled or disabled. Users can always view records they own.

B) Sharing rules override the option: Sharing rules can still be used to share records, even if the "Grant Access Using Hierarchies" option is disabled. However, the role hierarchy will not be considered for sharing purposes.

C) Only system administrators can access the records: This is not accurate. The level of access depends on the overall sharing settings and permissions of the users, not just the system administrator.

By understanding the role of the "Grant Access Using Hierarchies" option, you can effectively control data sharing within your Salesforce organization based on your specific security requirements.

6] Answer: D) All of the above

Explanation:

Salesforce offers various profiles to cater to different user roles and permissions within an organization. These profiles define the level of access users have to different objects, records, and functionalities.

- System Administrator: This profile grants the highest level of permissions, allowing full access to all Salesforce features and data.
- Standard User: This is the most common profile, providing access to standard sales, service, and marketing features.
- Read Only: This profile limits users to viewing data without being able to modify it.

By assigning the appropriate profile to each user, organizations can effectively manage security and ensure that users have the necessary access to perform their job functions.

Understanding the different profile types is essential for proper user provisioning and security management in Salesforce.

7] Answer: C) Login Access Policies

Explanation:

Login Access Policies control whether administrators can log in as any user in the organization.

To enable this feature, navigate to Setup > Security Controls > Login Access Policies. Check the box for Administrators Can Log in as Any User.

By enabling this option, administrators can easily troubleshoot user issues by logging in as the affected user to see the exact problem they're facing.

Why other options are incorrect:

- Login IP Restrictions are used to control access based on IP address, not for logging in as another user.
- Permission Sets are used to grant additional permissions to users, not for logging in as another user.
- Grant Login Access is a feature related to Marketing Cloud, not for standard Salesforce logins.

It's important to note that this feature should be used judiciously, as it can pose security risks if not handled carefully.

8] Answer: C) Manage Users

Explanation:

The Manage Users permission is specifically required to deactivate a user in Salesforce. This permission grants the necessary authority to manage user accounts within the organization, including activating, deactivating, and modifying user details.

While the System Administrator profile includes the Manage Users permission, it's not the only profile that can have this permission. Other custom profiles can also be granted the Manage Users permission to allow specific users to manage user accounts without full system administrator privileges.

Understanding the specific permissions required for various tasks is crucial for effective role-based access control in Salesforce.

9] B) Salesforce Platform

Explanation:

Salesforce Platform licenses offer the highest level of functionality and customization capabilities within the Salesforce ecosystem. They provide access to the full range of Salesforce features, including the ability to create up to 2,000 custom objects.

Salesforce licenses are primarily for sales and service users and have limitations on custom object creation.

Salesforce Identity is focused on identity management and doesn't include custom object creation capabilities.

Salesforce Chatter is a social collaboration tool and doesn't involve custom object creation.

Therefore, the Salesforce Platform license is the correct choice for organizations requiring extensive customization and object creation.

10] Answer: D) Alias

Explanation:

Username and Email are essential for user identification and authentication. They are mandatory fields.

Role is assigned to define a user's permissions and access levels within the organization. It is also a required field.

Alias is an optional field that can be used as an alternative name for the user. It's not mandatory for creating a new user.

Therefore, Alias is the field that is not mandatory when creating a new user in Salesforce.

11] D) All of the above

Explanation:

Customizes the Salesforce URL: My Domain allows you to replace the standard Salesforce subdomain (e.g., [invalid URL removed]) with a custom domain that aligns with your company's branding (e.g., [invalid URL removed]).

Enhances security with domain specific login: By using a custom domain, you can implement stricter security measures, such as enforcing specific domain names for logins, reducing the risk of phishing attacks.

Allows branding with custom logo and colors: While My Domain primarily focuses on URL customization, it also contributes to overall branding by providing a more consistent user experience with your company's identity.

In essence, My Domain is a powerful tool to enhance both the security and branding aspects of your Salesforce instance.

12] Correct Answer: A) Profiles control what users can do, while Permission Sets grant additional permissions

Explanation:

Profiles define the baseline permissions for a group of users. They determine what users can see, edit, create, and delete within the Salesforce org. Think of profiles as a foundation that establishes the core access level for a role.

Permission Sets are used to grant additional permissions on top of what is defined in a profile. They are more granular and can be used to assign specific permissions to users based on their job functions or responsibilities.

Why other options are incorrect:

B) Permission Sets control what users can do, while Profiles grant additional permissions: This is the opposite of how profiles and permission sets function.

C) Both are used to restrict access: While it's true that both can be used to restrict access, profiles provide a broader base of permissions, while permission sets are more granular and allow for finer control.

D) Profiles and Permission Sets cannot be used together: This is incorrect. Profiles and permission sets are often used together to provide a comprehensive and flexible access control model.

Example:

Imagine a sales organization. A "Sales Representative" profile might define basic permissions for accessing leads, contacts, and opportunities. However, some sales reps need additional permissions to create quotes. In this case, a "Quote Creation" permission set could be created and assigned to those specific reps, granting them the necessary permissions without affecting the permissions of other sales reps.

Additional Considerations:

Profiles are mandatory for every user, while permission sets are optional.

A user can have only one profile but can have multiple permission sets.

Permission sets are often used for specific tasks or functionalities, while profiles are typically aligned with job roles.

By understanding the fundamental differences between profiles and permission sets, you can effectively manage user access and security within your Salesforce organization.

13] Correct Answer: B) Record level access

Explanation:

Role Hierarchy defines the reporting relationships between users in an organization. It's used to automatically grant access to records owned by subordinates.

For instance, a manager can view and edit records owned by their subordinates, even if the manager doesn't have explicit sharing rules granting them access.

Why other options are incorrect:

A) Object permissions: Object permissions are controlled by profiles, not role hierarchies.

C) Field level security: Field level security is determined by field permissions on profiles and permission sets.

D) App access: App access is controlled by app permissions on profiles and permission sets.

Example:

Consider a sales organization with a hierarchical structure. A sales manager should be able to view and edit opportunities created by their sales representatives. By placing the sales manager in a higher role in the hierarchy than their representatives, the manager automatically gains access to their subordinates' opportunities.

Additional Considerations:

- Role hierarchies can be combined with sharing rules for more granular control over data access.
- It's essential to design the role hierarchy carefully to avoid unintended data exposure.
- Large and complex role hierarchies can impact performance.

By understanding how role hierarchies work, you can effectively manage data access and security in your Salesforce organization.

14] Correct Answer: A) Sharing Rules

Explanation:

Sharing Rules are used to determine who can access records that they don't own. Administrators can define specific criteria based on record fields, owner, or other factors to grant access to certain groups of users.

Why other options are incorrect:

B) Role Hierarchy: While role hierarchy grants access to records owned by subordinates, it doesn't allow for specific criteria-based sharing.

C) Organization Wide Defaults (OWDs): OWDs set the baseline access level for all records in an organization but don't provide granular control based on specific criteria.

D) Permission Sets: Permission sets grant additional permissions but don't control record-level sharing based on criteria.

Example:

Let's say a sales manager wants all sales reps to see opportunities that are close to closing. By creating a sharing rule based on the opportunity stage, the manager can grant access to all sales reps for opportunities in the "Closing" stage, even if they aren't owned by the sales rep.

Additional Considerations:

Sharing rules can be complex and should be carefully designed to avoid unintended data exposure.

There are two types of sharing rules: criteria-based and owner-based.

Sharing rules can be combined with role hierarchy and OWDs for a comprehensive data access strategy.

By effectively using sharing rules, administrators can ensure that the right people have access to the information they need while protecting sensitive data.

15] Correct Answer: D) Finance User

Explanation:

Standard Profiles are pre-built profiles that come with Salesforce, designed for common user roles. They include profiles like Standard User, Contract Manager, and Marketing User. These profiles offer a baseline set of permissions for specific user types.

Finance User is not a standard profile. It's likely a custom profile created to meet the specific needs of a finance department, granting permissions tailored to financial tasks and data access.

Additional Considerations:

While Salesforce offers a variety of standard profiles, organizations often create custom profiles to align with their unique business processes and security requirements.

Understanding the difference between standard and custom profiles is crucial for effective user management and access control.

16] Correct Answer: B) Opportunity

Explanation:

Opportunity is the standard Salesforce object specifically designed to manage potential revenue from sales. It tracks the sales process from initial contact to closing the deal.

Why other options are incorrect:

- Lead: A lead represents a potential customer before they become an opportunity.
- Account: An account is an organization or individual that a company does business with.
- Contact: A contact is an individual associated with an account.

Additional Considerations:

Opportunities contain fields like probability, close date, expected revenue, and stage, which help sales teams track and forecast potential deals.

Opportunities are often related to accounts, contacts, and leads through lookup relationships.

By effectively managing opportunities, sales teams can improve their forecasting accuracy, win rates, and overall sales performance.

17] Correct Answer: A) 500

Explanation:

The standard limit for custom fields per object in Salesforce is 500. However, this can vary depending on your Salesforce edition and other factors.

Additional Considerations:

While the standard limit is 500, it's important to note that exceeding this limit can impact performance.

Salesforce recommends carefully considering the necessity of each custom field to avoid creating unnecessary fields.

For objects with a large number of required fields, consider using a custom object to store related information.

By understanding the limitations on custom fields, you can optimize your Salesforce org's performance and maintain data integrity.

18] Correct Answer: C) Junction Object

Explanation:

Junction Object is specifically used to create a many-to-many relationship between two objects.

It acts as a bridge between the two objects, allowing multiple records in one object to be associated with multiple records in another object.

Why other options are incorrect:

Lookup Relationship: This creates a one-to-many relationship, meaning one record in one object can be associated with multiple records in another, but not vice versa.

- Master-Detail Relationship: This is a specialized type of lookup relationship where the child record (detail) is dependent on the parent record (master). It doesn't support many-to-many relationships.
- Hierarchical Relationship: This is used to create a parent-child hierarchy between records of the same object, not between different objects.

Example:

Consider a scenario where you want to track which products are included in different orders. You would create a junction object called "Order Product" with lookup relationships to both the "Order" and "Product" objects. This allows an order to have multiple products, and a product to be included in multiple orders.

By understanding the different types of relationships, you can effectively model complex data structures in Salesforce.

19] Correct Answer: D) Long Text Area

Explanation:

A unique field ensures that each record has a distinct value in that field.

Text fields, Email fields, and Number fields can all be made unique to enforce data integrity.

However, a Long Text Area field is designed to store large amounts of text, and it's unlikely that every record would have a completely unique value in this field. Therefore, it cannot be made a unique field.

By understanding the limitations of different field types, you can effectively design your Salesforce objects and maintain data quality.

20] Correct Answer: C) View and modify data model

Explanation:

Schema Builder is a visual tool in Salesforce that allows you to see and modify the structure of your data, including objects, fields, and relationships between them.

It provides a graphical representation of your Salesforce data model, making it easier to understand and manage.

Why other options are incorrect:

A) Import Data: Schema Builder is not used for importing data. This is typically done through data import wizards or APIs.

B) Build Reports: Reports are created using the Report Builder or Report Wizard, not the Schema Builder.

D) Deploy Apps: Deploying apps involves packaging and deployment tools, not the Schema Builder.

In essence, the Schema Builder is your go-to tool for designing and managing the underlying structure of your Salesforce data.

21] Correct Answer: A) Lead

Explanation:

Lead is the standard Salesforce object used to capture information about potential customers who have not yet been qualified as an opportunity. It's a record of a potential customer's interest in your products or services.

Why other options are incorrect:

- Account: Represents an organization or individual that is already a customer or partner.
- Opportunity: Represents a potential sale and is typically created from a qualified lead.
- Contact: Represents an individual associated with an account.

By effectively managing leads, sales teams can identify potential customers, nurture relationships, and convert them into opportunities.

22] Correct Answer: A) Lead Assignment Rules

Explanation:

Lead Assignment Rules are specifically designed to automate the process of assigning incoming leads to users or queues based on predefined criteria. These criteria can include lead source, industry, company size, geographic location, and more.

Why other options are incorrect:

- Lead Queues: While lead queues can be used to manage a group of leads, they don't automatically assign leads to users.
- Lead Workflow Rules: Workflow rules are used to automate actions based on record changes, but they are not specifically designed for lead assignment.
- Lead Scoring: Lead scoring is used to prioritize leads based on specific criteria but doesn't automatically assign leads to users.

By using Lead Assignment Rules, organizations can efficiently distribute incoming leads to the appropriate sales representatives, improving lead response times and increasing sales productivity.

23] Answer: A) 500

Explanation:

Salesforce imposes a daily limit of 500 leads that can be captured through Web-to-Lead. This limit is in place to ensure system performance and prevent abuse.

If your organization exceeds this limit, the Default Lead Creator (specified in the Web-to-Lead setup) receives an email containing the additional lead information.

Why other options are incorrect:

B) 1000, C) 2000, D) 5000: These options are incorrect as they exceed the actual limit of 500 leads per day for Web-to-Lead.

Additional Considerations:

While the daily limit is 500, it's important to note that this limit resets every 24 hours.

If you anticipate high lead volume, consider implementing lead routing rules or using third-party integration tools to manage lead distribution efficiently.

Salesforce offers additional features like lead scoring and assignment rules to prioritize and distribute leads effectively.

By understanding the Web-to-Lead limit and implementing appropriate strategies, you can optimize your lead management process and ensure that all incoming leads are captured and handled efficiently.

24] Answer: C) Attribute revenue to marketing campaigns

Explanation:

Campaign Influence is a powerful tool in Salesforce that helps you measure the impact of your marketing campaigns on revenue generation.

By associating opportunities with the campaigns that influenced them, you can accurately determine which marketing efforts are driving the most sales.

This data is crucial for making informed decisions about marketing budget allocation and campaign optimization.

Why other options are incorrect:

A) Track email campaigns: While Campaign Influence can be used to track the impact of email campaigns, it's a broader tool for measuring the influence of all marketing campaigns on revenue.

B) Track sales performance: Campaign Influence focuses on the marketing side of the equation, not sales performance.

D) Manage campaign members: Campaign members are associated with campaigns, but Campaign Influence goes beyond that by attributing revenue to specific campaigns.

Example:

Imagine a company launches three marketing campaigns: a social media campaign, an email campaign, and a webinar. By using Campaign Influence, they can determine which campaign contributed most to the closed opportunities and allocate their marketing budget accordingly.

Additional Considerations:

Campaign Influence works in conjunction with other Salesforce features like campaign hierarchy and lead sources to provide a comprehensive view of marketing performance.

There are two versions of Campaign Influence: Campaign Influence 1.0 and Customizable Campaign Influence. The latter offers more flexibility in assigning influence percentages to multiple campaigns.

By effectively using Campaign Influence, organizations can gain valuable insights into their marketing ROI and make data-driven decisions to improve their marketing strategy.

25] Answer: A) Company

Explanation:

Company is the only required field when converting a lead in Salesforce.

This information is essential for creating the corresponding account record during the conversion process.

Why other options are incorrect:

B) Email, C) Status, D) Phone: While these fields are important for lead management, they are not mandatory when converting a lead. Salesforce allows for flexibility in data collection and doesn't enforce these fields at the conversion stage.

Additional Considerations:

Even though Company is the only required field, it's highly recommended to populate as much information as possible about the lead before conversion. This includes fields like Email, Phone, and other relevant details.

You can customize the lead conversion process by defining required fields through validation rules or custom buttons. This allows you to enforce specific data requirements for your organization.

By understanding the required fields for lead conversion, you can ensure data consistency and improve the overall lead management process.

26] Answer: A) Case

Explanation:

Cases are specifically designed to manage customer support issues or inquiries within Salesforce. They provide a centralized location to track and resolve customer problems efficiently.

Cases include fields for capturing customer information, issue details, priorities, statuses, and other relevant data.

Why other options are incorrect:

B) Opportunity: Opportunities are used to track potential sales deals.

C) Lead: Leads represent potential customers who have not yet converted to opportunities.

D) Solution: Solutions are knowledge articles or FAQs that can be associated with cases but are not used to track individual issues.

Additional Considerations:

Salesforce offers various features to support case management, such as case escalation, case assignment, email-to-case, and case-related knowledge articles.

You can customize cases to fit your organization's specific support processes and requirements.

Integrating cases with other Salesforce objects, such as accounts and contacts, provides a holistic view of customer interactions.

By effectively utilizing cases, businesses can improve customer satisfaction, streamline support processes, and measure key performance indicators (KPIs) related to customer service.

27] Answer: A) Knowledge Base

Explanation:

Knowledge Base is Salesforce's built-in platform for creating, storing, and managing self-service articles. It allows users to search and browse articles based on keywords, categories, or other criteria.

This feature empowers customers and agents alike to find solutions independently, reducing case volume and improving overall efficiency.

Why other options are incorrect:

B) Solution Manager: While related to managing solutions, it doesn't provide a search and browse interface for users.

C) Article Management: This is an administrative function for managing articles within the Knowledge Base, not for user interaction.

D) Content Library: This term is not standard Salesforce terminology and doesn't accurately describe the feature in question.

Additional Considerations:

The Knowledge Base can be configured to display articles in various formats, such as lists, search results, or detailed pages.

It integrates seamlessly with other Salesforce features like cases and communities, providing a comprehensive self-service solution.

Effective use of the Knowledge Base requires careful article creation, categorization, and maintenance.

By leveraging the Knowledge Base, organizations can enhance customer satisfaction, reduce support costs, and empower employees with quick access to information.

28] Answer: A) Automatically assign cases to users or queues based on criteria

Explanation:

Case Assignment Rules are a powerful tool in Salesforce for automating the distribution of incoming cases to the appropriate agents or support teams.

By defining specific criteria, such as case type, origin, or account, you can create rules to automatically assign cases to the best-equipped individuals or queues.

Why other options are incorrect:

B) Track case resolution time: This is handled by case fields like created date, closed date, and time spent on case.

C) Escalate cases: While you can set up escalation rules, they are separate from case assignment rules.

D) Merge duplicate cases: This is a different process involving data management tools and functions.

Example:

A customer support department might have different teams for technical issues, billing inquiries, and general support. Using case assignment rules, incoming cases can be automatically routed to the correct team based on the case's subject or type.

Additional Considerations:

Case assignment rules can be combined with other features like queues and escalation rules for a comprehensive case management strategy.

Careful planning and testing are essential to ensure that cases are assigned correctly and efficiently.

By effectively utilizing case assignment rules, organizations can improve case handling efficiency, increase customer satisfaction, and optimize resource allocation.

29] Answer: D) Dashboard

Explanation:

The Service Cloud Console is a unified workspace designed to improve agent productivity and customer experience. It consists of several core components that work together to provide a streamlined interface for handling customer interactions.

List View, Interaction Log, and Utility Bar are all essential components of the Service Cloud Console.

Breakdown of components:

- List View: Displays a list of records (e.g., cases, contacts) that the agent is working on.
- Interaction Log: Provides a chronological record of interactions with a customer, including emails, calls, and chat transcripts.
- Utility Bar: Contains shortcuts to commonly used actions and tools, such as creating cases, logging calls, and accessing knowledge articles.

Why Dashboard is not a component:

While dashboards are valuable tools in Salesforce for visualizing data and performance metrics, they are not specifically designed as part of the Service Cloud Console's core interface. Dashboards are typically accessed separately to provide a broader overview of performance and trends.

By understanding the components of the Service Cloud Console, agents can efficiently manage their workload and provide excellent customer service.

30] Answer: B) Escalation Rules

Explanation:

Escalation Rules are specifically designed to automate the process of escalating cases based on predefined conditions.

You can set up rules to automatically escalate a case to a higher-level support team or individual if it remains open for a certain period.

This helps ensure timely resolution of cases and prevents customer dissatisfaction due to delays.

Why other options are incorrect:

A) Case Assignment Rules: These rules are used to assign cases to users or queues based on specific criteria but do not handle escalations.

C) Auto Response Rules: These are used to send automatic email responses based on case creation or updates, not for escalation purposes.

D) Validation Rules: These are used to enforce data integrity and prevent invalid data entry, unrelated to case escalation.

Additional Considerations:

Escalation rules can be based on various criteria, such as case age, priority, or specific case fields.

You can configure multiple escalation levels to define different escalation paths based on case severity or other factors.

Effective use of escalation rules requires careful planning and consideration of your organization's support processes.

By implementing escalation rules, you can improve case handling efficiency, enhance customer satisfaction, and ensure that critical cases receive the attention they require.

31] Answer: D) Note

Explanation:

Task, Event, and Call are the three standard activity types in Salesforce used to track interactions and to-dos related to accounts, contacts, leads, and opportunities.

Notes are not considered a standard activity type. They are primarily used for internal communication and collaboration, not for tracking interactions with external parties.

Additional Considerations:

While Notes are not activity types, they can be associated with records like accounts, contacts, and opportunities for reference.

Salesforce offers other features like Chatter for more robust internal communication and collaboration.

By understanding the difference between activity types and notes, you can effectively use Salesforce to manage your interactions and track important information.

32] Answer: A) Receive updates about the record in their Chatter feed

Explanation:

The Follow button on a Salesforce record allows users to subscribe to updates and activities related to that record.

Once a user follows a record, they will see updates, comments, tasks, and other changes made to the record in their Chatter feed.

This feature is essential for collaboration and staying informed about the progress of records.

Why other options are incorrect:

B) Edit the record: Editing a record requires specific permissions and is not related to following.

C) Delete the record: Deleting a record requires specific permissions and is not related to following.

D) Share the record with other users: Sharing a record involves using specific sharing settings and is not the function of the Follow button.

By following a record, users can stay updated on its status, collaborate with colleagues, and efficiently manage their work.

33] Answer: A) Chatter

Explanation:

Chatter is Salesforce's social collaboration platform that enables users to interact and collaborate on records. It allows for real-time communication, file sharing, and the ability to post comments and questions directly on records.

Why other options are incorrect:

B) Groups: While Groups can be used for collaboration, they are more focused on creating communities of users with shared interests rather than collaborating on specific records.

C) Teams: Salesforce doesn't have a standard feature called "Teams" for collaboration. There might be custom implementations or third-party apps using this term, but it's not a core Salesforce feature.

D) Feed Tracking: This refers to monitoring changes to a record's feed, but it doesn't facilitate collaboration among users.

By using Chatter, teams can work together effectively, share knowledge, and improve productivity on Salesforce records.

34] Answer: B) Schedule Events and Tasks

Explanation:

The Salesforce Calendar is a tool for managing your schedule and organizing your time. It allows you to create, edit, and view events and tasks, ensuring that you stay on top of your commitments.

You can schedule meetings, appointments, and other activities, set reminders, and integrate your calendar with other applications.

Why other options are incorrect:

A) Track Opportunities: Opportunities are tracked using the Opportunity object.

C) Manage Leads: Leads are managed using the Lead object.

D) Monitor Campaigns: Campaigns are tracked using the Campaign object.

By effectively using the Salesforce Calendar, users can improve time management, increase productivity, and better coordinate their activities.

35] Answer: C) Shared Activities

Explanation:

Shared Activities is the Salesforce feature that enables you to associate multiple contacts with a single event or task. This is particularly useful for meetings or tasks involving multiple stakeholders.

By using Shared Activities, you can track interactions with multiple contacts efficiently and maintain a clear record of who participated in an activity.

Why other options are incorrect:

A) Event Relations: This term is not a standard Salesforce feature.

B) Activity Linking: This term is also not a standard Salesforce feature.

D) Task Linking: While it's possible to link tasks to multiple records, it doesn't specifically address relating multiple contacts to a single task.

Shared Activities is the correct choice for associating multiple contacts with an event or task.

36] Answer: A) 2GB

Explanation:

The maximum file size for files uploaded to Salesforce is 2GB.

This limit applies to files uploaded directly through the user interface, as well as through various APIs.

Why other options are incorrect:

B) 5MB, C) 10MB, D) 25MB: These options are significantly lower than the actual maximum file size limit.

Additional Considerations:

While the maximum file size is 2GB, there might be limitations based on the specific feature or API being used. For example, email attachments might have smaller limits.

Salesforce offers features like Content and Salesforce Files for managing large files efficiently.

It's essential to consider file size limitations when designing file upload processes and user experiences.

By understanding the maximum file size limits, you can effectively manage file uploads and storage within Salesforce.

37] Answer: B) Import data from external sources

Explanation:

The Data Import Wizard is a tool in Salesforce used to transfer data from external sources into Salesforce objects. This process is often referred to as data migration or bulk import.

You can import data from various formats, such as CSV, Excel, and other delimited files, into standard and custom objects.

Why other options are incorrect:

A) Export Data: This is the opposite of importing data. Salesforce offers different tools for exporting data.

C) Sync data with other systems: While the Data Import Wizard can be used as part of a data synchronization process, it primarily focuses on the initial import of data.

D) Delete records: The Data Import Wizard is not designed for deleting records. You would use other tools or bulk APIs for this purpose.

By using the Data Import Wizard, you can efficiently populate your Salesforce org with data from external systems, saving time and effort compared to manual entry.

38] Regularly backing up your Salesforce data is crucial for disaster recovery and data integrity. Salesforce provides several tools for data export, but only one is specifically designed for scheduling backups.

Answer: D) Data Integrator

While Data Loader, Data Export, and Data Import Wizard are tools for data manipulation, Data Integrator is the correct answer for scheduling regular data backups.

Data Integrator is a powerful tool that allows you to automate data integration processes, including scheduling data exports. You can define schedules, export formats (CSV, Excel, etc.), and even specify data filters for your backups.

Why other options are incorrect:

A) Data Loader: Primarily used for bulk importing and exporting data, but it doesn't offer scheduling capabilities.

B) Data Export: This is a manual process for exporting data. It doesn't provide automated scheduling.

C) Data Import Wizard: Used for importing data into Salesforce, not for exporting or scheduling backups.

Additional considerations:

- Salesforce Backup: While not a direct answer to the question, it's worth mentioning that Salesforce offers a built-in backup solution called Salesforce Backup. However, it's a paid add-on and doesn't replace the need for regular data exports as an additional safeguard.
- Data Export Frequency: The frequency of your backups depends on your organization's data volume, criticality, and compliance requirements. It's essential to establish a backup schedule that meets your specific needs.

By utilizing Data Integrator for scheduled data backups, you can ensure that your Salesforce data is protected and readily available in case of data loss or corruption.

39] Duplicate records can lead to data inconsistencies and errors. Salesforce provides tools to identify and merge these duplicates, improving data quality and efficiency.

Answer: A) Duplicate Management

Duplicate Management is the overarching feature in Salesforce that encompasses all aspects of handling duplicate records. It includes tools like duplicate rules, matching rules, and duplicate jobs to identify and merge duplicates.

Why other options are incorrect:

B) Data Cleansing: While related to data quality, data cleansing is a broader term that includes various activities to improve data accuracy, such as removing duplicates, correcting errors, and standardizing data formats.

C) Data Quality: This is a general concept referring to the overall accuracy and consistency of data. It includes duplicate management as a component.

D) Duplicate Rules: Duplicate rules are a specific tool within Duplicate Management. They define the criteria for identifying potential duplicates.

Additional considerations:

- Matching Rules: These rules determine how Salesforce compares records to identify potential duplicates.
- Duplicate Jobs: These jobs scan your data for duplicates based on defined matching rules.
- Merge Rules: These rules specify how data from duplicate records is combined when merging.

By effectively utilizing Duplicate Management features, you can maintain data integrity, improve data quality, and enhance overall Salesforce performance.

40] Answer: C) 50,000

The Data Import Wizard in Salesforce has a limit of 50,000 records per import. This is a standard limitation to ensure efficient data processing and system performance.

Why other options are incorrect:

A) 10,000, B) 20,000, and D) 100,000 are incorrect as they do not match the actual limit.

Additional considerations:

- Large Data Imports: For importing more than 50,000 records, consider using Data Loader or the Bulk API, which can handle larger data volumes.
- Data Quality: Regardless of the import method, always prioritize data quality and cleansing before importing to avoid issues.
- Import Performance: Large imports can impact system performance. It's advisable to schedule them during off-peak hours.

By understanding the limitations of the Data Import Wizard and utilizing appropriate tools for larger data sets, you can efficiently manage data imports in Salesforce.

41] Answer: A) A template for creating reports

Explanation:

A Report Type in Salesforce is essentially a blueprint that defines the structure of a report. It determines which objects and fields will be available when creating a report. Think of it as a pre-configured framework that you can use to build different reports based on your specific needs.

Why other options are incorrect:

B) A way to schedule reports: This is incorrect. Report scheduling is a separate feature that allows you to automate report generation and distribution.

C) A filter for report data: While you can filter data within a report, the Report Type itself does not define filters. Filters are applied when building a specific report based on a Report Type.

D) A report sharing setting: Report sharing settings control who can access and view specific reports. Report Types are unrelated to sharing permissions.

Additional Considerations:

- Standard Report Types: Salesforce provides several standard Report Types out of the box, covering common reporting needs (e.g., Accounts & Contacts, Opportunities with Products).
- Custom Report Types: You can create custom Report Types to meet specific reporting requirements that aren't covered by standard options.
- Report Types and Objects: A Report Type always includes a primary object and can optionally include related objects.

By understanding Report Types, you can efficiently create and manage reports in Salesforce, gaining valuable insights into your data.

42] Answer: A) Dashboards

Explanation:

Dashboards are the primary tool for visualizing data in Salesforce. They provide a consolidated view of key performance indicators (KPIs) and trends through various chart types like bar graphs, pie charts, line charts, and more. Dashboards can display data from multiple reports, making it easy to analyze and understand complex information at a glance.

Why other options are incorrect:

B) Reports: Reports provide data in tabular format. While they can be the source data for dashboards, they themselves don't offer graphical visualizations.

C) Charts: Charts are a component of dashboards. They display data in a visual format within a dashboard.

D) Analytics: Analytics is a broader term encompassing data analysis, reporting, and forecasting. While it includes visualization, dashboards are the specific tool for creating visual representations of data.

Additional Considerations:

- Dashboard Components: Dashboards can include various components beyond charts, such as tables, metrics, and filters.
- Customizing Dashboards: You can customize dashboards to fit specific user roles and needs by selecting appropriate reports and chart types.
- Interactive Dashboards: Some dashboards can be made interactive, allowing users to drill down into data for further analysis.

By effectively utilizing dashboards, you can transform raw data into actionable insights and make informed business decisions.

43] Answer: There is no strict limit on the number of reports you can add to a dashboard in Salesforce.

While there's technically no defined maximum, it's essential to consider the following:

- Dashboard performance: Too many reports on a single dashboard can impact performance.
- Visual clutter: Overloading a dashboard with reports can make it difficult to read and understand.
- User experience: A cluttered dashboard can be overwhelming for users.

Best practices:

- Focus on key metrics: Prioritize the most important information for your users.
- Organize dashboards: Create multiple dashboards for different audiences or purposes.
- Use dashboard components effectively: Combine charts, tables, and metrics for a balanced view.

By following these guidelines, you can create effective dashboards that provide valuable insights without compromising performance or user experience.

44] Answer: D) All of the above

Salesforce provides multiple methods to share reports with other users:

- Report Sharing Settings: This is the most granular method, allowing you to specify exact sharing permissions for individual users or groups of users on a specific report. You can grant different levels of access, such as view, edit, or run the report.

- Folder Sharing: By sharing a folder containing the report, you can grant access to multiple reports at once. This is efficient when you want to share a group of related reports.
- Report Link: Generating a report link allows you to share a specific report with anyone, even external users, without requiring Salesforce access. However, this method doesn't provide granular control over report actions.

By understanding these options, you can choose the most appropriate method based on your specific sharing requirements and the level of access you want to grant to other users.

45Answer: C) Histogram

Explanation:

While Salesforce offers a variety of chart types for data visualization, histograms are not among them.

Available chart types in Salesforce:

- Line Chart: Displays data points connected by lines, often used to show trends over time.
- Bar Chart: Represents data using rectangular bars, suitable for comparisons.
- Funnel Chart: Illustrates a process or workflow with stages represented by decreasingly sized shapes.

Histograms are typically used in statistical analysis to visualize the distribution of numerical data. While they are valuable tools for data interpretation, Salesforce doesn't currently provide a built-in option for creating histograms.

46] Answer: B) A feature to automate business processes

Explanation:

A Workflow Rule in Salesforce is a powerful tool that allows you to automate various business processes based on specific criteria. It acts as a set of instructions that Salesforce follows when certain conditions are met within a record.

Why other options are incorrect:

A) A tool to import data: While Salesforce offers tools for data import, Workflow Rules are not specifically designed for this purpose.

C) A report customization tool: Reports are customized using filters, group by options, and report types, not Workflow Rules.

D) A way to manage user permissions: User permissions are managed through profiles and permission sets. Workflow Rules focus on automating actions within records.

Examples of Workflow Rule use cases:

- Automatically assigning leads to sales reps based on lead source.
- Sending email notifications when an opportunity reaches a specific stage.
- Updating a custom field based on the value of another field.
- Creating tasks or events when specific conditions are met.

By effectively using Workflow Rules, you can streamline your business processes, improve efficiency, and reduce manual effort.

47] Answer: D) Validation Rules

Explanation:

A Workflow Rule consists of three main components:

- Criteria: The conditions that must be met for the workflow to execute.
- Actions: The steps to be taken when the criteria are met.
- Time Triggers: (Optional) Specifies when the workflow rule should be evaluated.

Validation Rules are separate features in Salesforce used to enforce data integrity by preventing invalid data from being saved. They are not part of Workflow Rules.

48] Answer: D) All of the above

Workflow Rules are versatile tools that can perform a variety of actions when specific criteria are met. These actions include:

- Create Task: Automatically generates a task for a user or group.
- Send Email Alert: Sends an email notification to specified recipients.
- Update Field: Modifies the value of a field on a record.

By combining these actions, you can create complex automated processes to streamline your business operations.

49] Answer: C) Automate complex business processes

Explanation:

Process Builder is a powerful tool in Salesforce used to automate complex business processes. It allows you to create automated actions based on specific criteria or events. For example, you can:

- Send email alerts when a lead becomes an opportunity.
- Create tasks for sales reps to follow up on opportunities.
- Update record fields based on certain conditions.
- Escalate cases to different support levels based on priority.
- Initiate approvals for specific record types.

By automating these processes, you can significantly improve efficiency, reduce errors, and free up your team's time to focus on more strategic tasks.

Why other options are incorrect:

A) Import data: This is typically handled by data import wizards or tools like Data Loader.

B) Create records: While Process Builder can create records as part of an automated process, it's not its primary purpose.

D) Manage profiles: Profiles are used to control user access and permissions, which is a separate administrative task.

Example: Imagine a sales process where, once an opportunity reaches a certain stage and its value exceeds a specific threshold, you want to create a task for the sales manager to review the opportunity and send an email to the customer. Using Process Builder, you can set up a process to automatically create the task and send the email when these conditions are met.

Additional Considerations:

While Process Builder is a valuable tool, for more complex automation scenarios, consider using Flow Builder, which offers greater flexibility and features.

It's essential to design your processes carefully to avoid performance issues.

Regularly review and optimize your Process Builders to ensure they continue to meet your business needs.

50] Answer: B) Approval Processes

Explanation:

Approval Processes are specifically designed to manage multi-step approval workflows within Salesforce. They provide a structured way to route records through a series of approval steps, involving multiple approvers, based on defined criteria.

You can configure approval processes with:

- Multiple approval steps: Each step can have different criteria, approvers, and actions.
- Different approval paths: You can create multiple approval paths based on specific conditions.
- Escalation rules: If an approval is not completed within a specified time, the process can be escalated to another approver.
- Notifications: Email and in-app notifications can be sent to approvers and record owners.

Why other options are incorrect:

A) Workflow Rules: While Workflow Rules can automate actions based on record changes, they are not designed for complex approval processes.

C) Validation Rules: Validation Rules enforce data integrity by preventing invalid data from being saved, not for managing approvals.

D) Process Builder: While Process Builder can automate various processes, it's not the primary tool for managing multi-step approvals.

Example: A company might have a multi-step approval process for expense reports. First, the manager approves expenses up to a certain amount. For larger expenses, the approval process might require additional approvals from the finance department and executive management. Approval Processes can be configured to handle this complex workflow efficiently.

Additional Considerations:

Approval Processes can be used for various record types, such as opportunities, contracts, and custom objects.

Consider using approval queues to manage a pool of approvers for specific types of records.

Regularly review and optimize your approval processes to ensure they align with your business requirements.

51Answer: D) All of the above

Explanation:

Salesforce1 is a powerful mobile app that offers a robust platform for accessing and managing Salesforce data on the go.

- Offline access to data: Salesforce1 allows users to continue working with data even when there's no internet connection. This is crucial for sales reps, field service technicians, and other mobile users who need to access information while on the move.
- Access to custom objects: Any custom objects created in your Salesforce org can be accessed through the Salesforce1 mobile app. This ensures that mobile users have access to the same data as desktop users.
- Mobile-only features: Salesforce1 offers features specifically designed for mobile use, such as mobile-optimized layouts, touch-based interactions, and integration with device capabilities like camera and GPS.

By combining these features, Salesforce1 empowers users to be productive and connected, regardless of their location.

Example: A field service technician can use the Salesforce1 app to access customer information, create service reports, and update case statuses even when they are on-site and without internet connectivity.

Additional Considerations:

Consider optimizing your Salesforce1 app for different device sizes and screen orientations to provide the best user experience.

Utilize mobile-specific features like location services and push notifications to enhance the app's functionality.

Regularly test the app on different devices to ensure optimal performance and compatibility.

52] Answer: A) Build custom mobile apps

Explanation:

Mobile Publisher is a Salesforce tool that allows you to create custom mobile apps without requiring extensive coding knowledge. It enables you to:

- Customize the Salesforce mobile app: Modify the look and feel of the app to match your company's branding.
- Select specific features: Choose the features and functionality you want to include in your app based on your users' needs.

- Distribute the app: Publish your custom app to app stores for easy distribution to your employees or customers.

Why other options are incorrect:

B) Create mobile responsive pages: This is typically achieved using Lightning components and themes.

C) Publish mobile content: Mobile Publisher focuses on creating the app itself, not just publishing content within it.

D) Manage mobile notifications: While Mobile Publisher can be integrated with notification services, its primary purpose is app creation.

Example: A sales organization might use Mobile Publisher to create a custom mobile app that includes features like lead management, opportunity tracking, and sales forecasting. The app can be branded with the company's logo and colors, providing a consistent user experience for sales reps.

Additional Considerations:

Mobile Publisher can help improve user adoption of Salesforce by providing a tailored mobile experience.

Consider using analytics to track app usage and identify areas for improvement.

Regularly update your app to ensure it meets the evolving needs of your users.

53] Answer: D) Search Layout

Explanation:

While Salesforce1 offers a high degree of customization, Search Layout is not a customizable field for the mobile app. The search functionality on mobile is designed for quick and efficient searches, and the search layout is optimized for this purpose.

Why other options are incorrect:

A) Compact Layout: You can customize compact layouts to display specific fields on mobile devices for efficient data entry and viewing.

B) Record Pages: You can create custom record pages for mobile devices to tailor the user interface and optimize the layout for smaller screens.

C) List Views: You can customize list views to display specific columns and filter records for mobile users, providing a relevant view of data.

By understanding these customization options, Salesforce administrators can create a mobile experience that is tailored to the specific needs of their users.

54] Answer: C) Perform quick actions on mobile

Explanation:

Mobile Smart Actions are designed to streamline workflows and increase productivity on mobile devices. They provide a quick and easy way to perform common actions directly from the Salesforce1 mobile app without navigating through multiple screens.

Examples of Mobile Smart Actions include:

- Creating new records (e.g., creating a new opportunity from a lead)
- Updating record fields (e.g., changing an opportunity stage)
- Logging calls or sending emails
- Approving or rejecting records

Why other options are incorrect:

A) Automate mobile data entry: While Mobile Smart Actions can speed up data entry, they don't automate the entire process.

B) Enable voice commands: Salesforce does offer voice commands through integration with voice assistants, but this is a separate feature.

D) Sync mobile data: Salesforce automatically syncs data between the mobile app and the cloud.

By using Mobile Smart Actions, users can save time and improve efficiency while on the go.

55] Answer: C) Salesforce1 Notifications

Explanation:

Salesforce1 Notifications is the feature that enables push notifications to be sent to mobile devices. It allows you to deliver timely and relevant information to users, even when they're not actively using the Salesforce1 app.

These notifications can be triggered based on specific events or criteria, such as:

- Record updates (e.g., a case status change)
- Task assignments

- Approvals
- Custom events

Why other options are incorrect:

A) Chatter: While Chatter is used for internal communication, it doesn't specifically handle push notifications.

B) Mobile Alerts: This term isn't a standard Salesforce feature.

D) Workflow Alerts: Workflow Alerts are primarily used for email notifications, not push notifications.

Example: A sales rep can receive a push notification when a new lead is assigned to them, allowing them to quickly follow up.

By leveraging Salesforce1 Notifications, organizations can improve communication, increase user engagement, and drive productivity.

56] Answer: A) A marketplace for Salesforce apps

Explanation:

AppExchange is Salesforce's online marketplace where you can find and install a wide range of applications, components, and services that extend the functionality of your Salesforce platform. It's like an app store for Salesforce, offering solutions for various business needs.

Think of it as a one-stop shop for businesses to discover and implement pre-built applications without the need to develop everything from scratch.

Why other options are incorrect:

B) A tool for data integration: While AppExchange can include apps for data integration, it's not its primary function.

C) A community forum: Salesforce has a community forum, but it's separate from AppExchange.

D) A reporting tool: Salesforce offers built-in reporting tools, and while some AppExchange apps might enhance reporting capabilities, it's not its core purpose.

57] Answer: D) Scripts

Explanation:

AppExchange offers a variety of pre-built solutions and components to enhance Salesforce functionality. These typically include:

- Apps: Complete, standalone applications that address specific business needs.
- Components: Individual building blocks like Lightning components, Apex classes, or Visual force pages that can be used to customize Salesforce.
- Solutions: Bundles of apps, components, and services that provide comprehensive solutions for specific industries or departments.

Scripts are not a standard component type on AppExchange. They are usually custom-developed code written by developers for specific purposes within a Salesforce org.

58] Answer: C) Directly from the AppExchange interface

Explanation:

AppExchange is designed to provide a seamless user experience for installing apps. You can directly search for, select, and install an app from within the AppExchange platform. The process involves:

- Browsing or searching for the desired app.
- Selecting the app and clicking on the "Get It Now" button.
- Choosing the installation environment (production or sandbox).
- Reviewing and accepting terms and conditions.
- Confirming the installation.

Why other options are incorrect:

A) Using the Data Import Wizard: This tool is primarily used for importing data into Salesforce, not for installing apps.

B) By downloading and manually uploading: While this method might have been possible in earlier Salesforce versions, it's not the standard or recommended approach nowadays.

D) Via a third party service: AppExchange is the official marketplace for Salesforce apps, and using third-party services for installation is generally not recommended.

By installing apps directly from AppExchange, you ensure that the app is compatible with your Salesforce org and that you have access to necessary support and updates.

59] Answer: D) All of the above

Explanation:

AppExchange offers a multitude of benefits for Salesforce users:

- Prebuilt functionalities: AppExchange apps provide ready-made solutions for various business needs, saving time and resources compared to building everything from scratch.
- Reduced development time: By utilizing pre-built components and apps, organizations can significantly reduce development time and costs.
- Access to a wider range of tools: AppExchange offers a vast ecosystem of solutions, providing access to tools and features that might not be available in standard Salesforce.

Leveraging AppExchange can accelerate business processes, improve efficiency, and enhance overall Salesforce utilization.

60] Answer: C) A type of app that can be updated by the provider

Explanation:

A Managed Package is a container that includes the components of a Salesforce application, and it's a mechanism for installing apps in Salesforce orgs. Essentially, it's a pre-built application that can be distributed and installed by other Salesforce users.

Key characteristics:

- Pre-built functionality: Includes a collection of pre-built components like objects, fields, workflows, etc.
- Upgradability: The package provider can release updates and improvements to the package, which can be installed by customers.
- Controlled environment: The package is tightly controlled by the provider, limiting customization options for the end-user.
- Distribution: Often distributed through AppExchange.

Why other options are incorrect:

A) A collection of prebuilt functionalities: While this is partially true, it doesn't capture the essence of a managed package's upgradability and controlled nature.

B) A set of API integrations: Managed packages can include API integrations, but they are not limited to this.

118

D) A bundle of reports and dashboards: While managed packages can include reports and dashboards, they are much more comprehensive than that.

In essence, a Managed Package is a packaged application that can be installed and managed by the provider, offering a controlled and upgradable solution for Salesforce users.

61] Answer: A) It provides a unified view of customer interactions

Explanation:

The Service Cloud Console is designed to offer a centralized workspace for customer service agents to manage and resolve customer issues efficiently. It brings together all relevant information about a customer, including cases, accounts, contacts, and related records, into a single view. This enables agents to have a comprehensive understanding of the customer's history and quickly address their needs.

Why other options are incorrect:

B) It is used to manage marketing campaigns: This is the function of Marketing Cloud.

C) It allows for direct integration with financial software: While Service Cloud can integrate with various systems, direct integration with financial software is not its primary focus.

D) It is used to develop custom apps: This is the purpose of the Salesforce Platform, not the Service Cloud Console.

By providing a unified view of customer interactions, the Service Cloud Console empowers agents to deliver exceptional customer service.

62] Answer: B) Store and share articles and FAQs

Explanation:

The Knowledge object in Salesforce is specifically designed to create and manage a knowledge base. This includes storing articles, FAQs, and other relevant information that can be accessed by both customers and agents. By utilizing the Knowledge object, organizations can:

- Improve customer service: Provide customers with self-service options, reducing case volume and improving response times.
- Empower agents: Equip support agents with quick access to information, enabling them to resolve issues efficiently.

- Centralize knowledge: Maintain a single repository for all company knowledge, ensuring consistency and accuracy.
- Measure knowledge effectiveness: Track article views, ratings, and case deflection rates to evaluate knowledge base performance.

Why other options are incorrect:

A) Store and manage customer cases: Cases are managed using the Case object.

C) Track sales opportunities: Opportunities are tracked using the Opportunity object.

D) Manage service contracts: Salesforce offers specific tools for managing contracts, but the Knowledge object is not primarily for this purpose.

By effectively utilizing the Knowledge object, organizations can create a valuable resource for both customers and employees.

63] Answer: A) Case Assignment Rules

Explanation:

Case Assignment Rules are specifically designed to automate the process of assigning cases to the appropriate agents or queues based on predefined criteria. These rules can be based on various factors such as:

- Case owner: Assigning cases to the owner of the related account or contact.
- Case subject or description: Routing cases based on keywords or specific criteria.
- Case origin: Directing cases from different channels (email, phone, web) to different teams.
- Case priority or urgency: Assigning high-priority cases to experienced agents or escalation teams.
- Case queue: Distributing cases evenly among a group of agents.

By using Case Assignment Rules, organizations can ensure that cases are efficiently routed to the best-equipped agents, improving response times and customer satisfaction.

Why other options are incorrect:

B) Case Auto Response Rules: These rules are used to automatically send email responses to customers when cases are created or updated.

C) Escalation Rules: Escalation Rules are used to automatically escalate cases to different levels of support based on specific criteria.

D) Case Queues: Case Queues are used to group cases together for assignment purposes, but they don't automatically route cases to specific agents.

64] Answer: B) A timeline of case activities

Explanation:

A Case Feed is a dynamic timeline that provides a chronological record of all activities related to a specific case. It serves as a central hub for collaboration and communication among support agents, customers, and other stakeholders involved in the case.

Key features of a Case Feed:

- Activity stream: Displays a chronological list of updates, comments, attachments, emails, and other interactions related to the case.
- Collaboration: Allows multiple users to participate in the case by adding comments, sharing files, and assigning tasks.
- Contextual information: Provides a comprehensive view of the case, including case details, related records, and customer information.
- Efficiency: Helps agents quickly access case history and relevant information to resolve issues effectively.

By leveraging the Case Feed, support teams can improve case handling, enhance customer satisfaction, and foster better collaboration within the team.

65] Answer: A) Track key stages in a case resolution process

Explanation:

Milestones in Salesforce are used to track specific stages or key points in a case's lifecycle. They help measure progress, set expectations, and ensure timely resolution of customer issues.

By defining milestones, you can:

- Monitor case progress: Track when certain steps in the case resolution process are completed.
- Set service level agreements (SLAs): Establish expected timelines for different stages of the case.
- Identify bottlenecks: Pinpoint areas where cases are delayed.

- Measure performance: Analyze milestone data to evaluate team performance and identify improvement opportunities.

Why other options are incorrect:

B) Manage marketing campaign timelines: This is typically handled with campaign management tools.

C) Monitor sales pipeline stages: Sales pipelines are managed through opportunity stages.

D) Schedule data backup operations: Salesforce has dedicated tools for data backup and management.

Milestones are specifically designed to enhance case management and improve customer satisfaction.

66] Answer: B) Calendar

Explanation:

The Calendar in Salesforce is the primary tool for scheduling and managing tasks and events. It provides a visual interface to view, create, edit, and delete appointments, meetings, and to-do lists.

Users can also:

- Set reminders and alerts for tasks and events
- View multiple calendars simultaneously
- Integrate with external calendars (like Google or Outlook)
- Relate tasks and events to other Salesforce records (like contacts, accounts, opportunities)

While the other options mentioned have related functionalities, the Calendar is the core feature dedicated to time management within Salesforce.

67] Answer: A) Real-time collaboration and information sharing

Explanation:

Chatter is Salesforce's built-in social collaboration tool. Its primary function is to facilitate real-time communication and information exchange among users within an organization. It's designed to foster a collaborative environment where employees can share ideas, updates, files, and knowledge quickly and efficiently.

Why other options are incorrect:

B) Task management: While Chatter can be used to track tasks to some extent, it's not its primary function. Salesforce has dedicated tools like Tasks and Projects for comprehensive task management.

C) Case resolution: Chatter can be used to collaborate on case solutions, but it's not specifically designed for case resolution. Salesforce has the Case object for managing customer support issues.

D) Data backup: Chatter is not a data backup solution. Salesforce has backup and restore features for data protection.

Additional considerations:

Chatter can significantly improve employee productivity and knowledge sharing.

It can be used to create a company culture of collaboration and innovation.

Chatter can be integrated with other Salesforce features like records, groups, and files.

Example: A sales team can use Chatter to share lead information, discuss sales strategies, and collaborate on deals in real-time, leading to improved sales performance.

68] Answer: C) By clicking the Follow button

Explanation:

To stay updated on changes to a specific record, a user must follow that record. This action subscribes the user to receive notifications and updates about the record in their Chatter feed.

Why other options are incorrect:

A) By liking the record: Liking a record indicates preference but doesn't subscribe you to updates.

B) By commenting on the record: Commenting on a record starts a conversation but doesn't automatically provide updates on record changes.

D) By sharing the record: Sharing a record distributes information but doesn't guarantee updates on the original record.

Additional considerations:

- Users can follow multiple records.
- Following a record doesn't automatically follow all related records.
- Users can unfollow records at any time.

Example: A sales rep wants to stay informed about a specific opportunity. By clicking the "Follow" button on the opportunity record, they will receive updates in their Chatter feed about changes to the opportunity, such as stage changes, amount changes, or new comments.

69] Answer: A) Organize users into collaborative groups

Explanation:

Chatter Groups are used to bring together a specific set of users who share common interests or work on the same projects. They provide a focused space for collaboration, information sharing, and discussion around a particular topic or project.

Why other options are incorrect:

B) Manage user permissions: Chatter Groups do not manage user permissions. Salesforce has a separate permission system for controlling user access to data and features.

C) Schedule tasks and events: While Chatter Groups can be used to discuss tasks and events, they are not specifically designed for scheduling. Salesforce has dedicated tools like Tasks and Events for scheduling.

D) Track sales opportunities: Chatter Groups can be used to collaborate on sales opportunities, but they are not primarily for tracking sales opportunities. Salesforce has the Opportunity object for tracking sales deals.

Additional considerations:

Chatter Groups can be public, private, or unlisted.

They can be used to share files, links, and other content.

Chatter Groups can be used to create a sense of community within an organization.

Example: A marketing team can create a Chatter Group to discuss upcoming campaigns, share marketing materials, and collaborate on projects.

70] Answer: A) Chatter Direct

Explanation:

Chatter Direct is the feature within Salesforce that enables users to send private messages to other individuals. It allows for one-on-one or group conversations, providing a secure channel for confidential communication.

Why other options are incorrect:

B) Chatter Messenger: There is no standard Salesforce feature called Chatter Messenger.

C) Chatter Connect: This term is not associated with any specific Salesforce functionality.

D) Chatter Private: While "private" might suggest direct messaging, the actual feature is called Chatter Direct.

Additional considerations:

Chatter Direct messages are not visible to other users unless they are added to the conversation.

Users can search for previous Chatter Direct messages.

Chatter Direct is a valuable tool for confidential communication within an organization.

Example: A sales rep needs to send sensitive customer information to a colleague. They can use Chatter Direct to securely share the information without exposing it to other users.

71] Answer: D) All of the above

Explanation:

Data Loader is a powerful tool in Salesforce for managing large volumes of data efficiently. It offers a versatile set of capabilities:

Import large volumes of data: Data Loader can handle importing massive datasets into Salesforce, often more efficiently than the user interface.

Export data to external systems: It can extract data from Salesforce and export it to various formats (CSV, Excel, etc.) for analysis or integration with other systems.

Perform bulk data updates: Data Loader allows for updating multiple records simultaneously, saving time and effort compared to manual updates.

Additional considerations:

Data Loader is a command-line tool, requiring some technical proficiency.

It's essential to validate data before importing to prevent errors.

Salesforce also offers other data management tools like Bulk API and Data Import Wizard for specific use cases.

Example: A company needs to migrate thousands of customer records from a legacy system to Salesforce. They can use Data Loader to import the data efficiently and accurately.

72] Answer: A) Data Export Service

Explanation:

Data Export Service is specifically designed for creating data backup files in Salesforce. It allows you to export data in a structured format, which can be used to restore data in case of data loss or corruption.

Why other options are incorrect:

B) Data Import Wizard: Used for importing data into Salesforce, not exporting for backup purposes.

C) Schema Builder: Primarily for designing the structure of your Salesforce data, not for exporting data.

D) Report Builder: Used for creating reports based on existing data, not for creating data backups.

Additional considerations:

Data Export Service can be scheduled for regular backups.

It's essential to have a robust data backup strategy in place.

Consider using external storage for backup files.

Example: A company implements a weekly data backup schedule using Data Export Service to protect their critical Salesforce data from accidental deletion or system failures.

73] Answer: A) A rule to identify duplicate records

Explanation:

A Matching Rule in Salesforce is a set of criteria used to determine whether two records are potential duplicates. It defines how Salesforce compares fields within records to identify potential matches.

Why other options are incorrect:

B) A rule to merge duplicate records: This is done by a Duplicate Rule, which is used in conjunction with a Matching Rule.

C) A rule to update records: This is achieved through Workflow Rules or Process Builder.

D) A rule to import records: Data Import Wizard or Data Loader is used for importing records.

Additional considerations:

Matching Rules are essential for maintaining data quality.

They can be created for standard objects like Accounts, Contacts, and Leads, as well as custom objects.

Multiple Matching Rules can be defined for a single object.

Example: A company wants to prevent duplicate contacts from being created. They create a Matching Rule based on email address, phone number, and first and last name to identify potential duplicates.

74] Answer: D) Opportunities

Explanation:

The Data Import Wizard is a user-friendly tool for importing data into Salesforce, but it has limitations. While it can handle standard objects like Accounts, Contacts, and Leads, it does not support Opportunities.

For importing Opportunities, you would typically use the Data Loader or the Bulk API, which offer more flexibility and control over the import process.

Additional considerations:

The Data Import Wizard is suitable for smaller data sets and users with limited technical expertise.

For larger data sets or more complex import requirements, Data Loader or Bulk API are recommended.

Example: A company wants to import a large list of new leads into Salesforce. They can use the Data Import Wizard for this task. However, if they also need to import associated opportunities, they would need to use Data Loader or Bulk API.

75] Answer: B) Duplicate Rules

Explanation:

Duplicate Rules are specifically designed to prevent the creation of duplicate records in Salesforce. They work in conjunction with Matching Rules which define the criteria for identifying potential duplicates. When a user attempts to create a record that matches an existing record based on the Duplicate Rule, *Salesforce can either*:

Display a warning to the user

Prevent the creation of the duplicate record

Merge the new record with the existing one

Why other options are incorrect:

A) Validation Rules: Used for enforcing data integrity by checking data accuracy and completeness, but not specifically for duplicates.

C) Workflow Rules: Automate actions based on record changes, not designed for duplicate prevention.

D) Escalation Rules: Used to assign tasks or send notifications based on specific conditions, unrelated to duplicate records.

Additional considerations:

Duplicate Rules can be created for standard and custom objects.

Multiple Duplicate Rules can be defined for a single object.

Effective use of Duplicate Rules requires careful consideration of matching criteria.

Example: A company wants to prevent duplicate contacts from being created. They create a Duplicate Rule based on email address and phone number. When a user tries to create a contact with an existing email or phone number, Salesforce will display a warning to prevent the duplicate.

76] Answer: B) Define the objects and fields available for reporting

Explanation:

A Custom Report Type in Salesforce is a blueprint that determines which objects and fields are included in a report. It essentially defines the data that can be displayed in a report. By creating custom report types, you can tailor the reporting capabilities to specific business needs.

Why other options are incorrect:

A) Customize the layout of a report: While you can customize the layout of a report after creating it, the custom report type defines the underlying data structure.

C) Set report filters: Filters are applied to a report based on the data defined in the custom report type, but they are not part of the report type itself.

D) Share reports with users: Report sharing is a separate function that controls who can access a report.

Additional considerations:

Custom report types are essential for complex reporting scenarios involving multiple objects.

They can improve report performance by reducing the amount of data processed.

Effective use of custom report types can enhance data analysis and decision-making.

Example: A sales team wants to create a report that shows opportunities, related contacts, and account information in a single view. They would create a custom report type that includes these objects and the necessary fields.

77] Answer: B) Report Filters

Explanation:

Report Filters provide the ability to dynamically filter report data based on specific criteria. Users can create and modify filters to view different subsets of data without having to create entirely new reports.

Why other options are incorrect:

A) Custom Report Types define the structure of a report, not the data it displays.

C) Dynamic Dashboards display real-time or historical data, but they don't filter report data directly.

D) Report Snapshots are static images of a report at a specific point in time, and they don't allow for dynamic filtering.

Additional considerations:

Report filters can be based on various criteria, including date ranges, record ownership, field values, and more.

Users can create multiple filters for a single report and switch between them easily.

Effective use of report filters can improve data analysis and decision-making.

Example: A sales manager wants to see a report of all closed-won opportunities in the last quarter. They can create a report filter based on the close date and opportunity stage to quickly view the desired data.

78] Answer: A) A report that groups data and provides subtotals

Explanation:

A Summary Report in Salesforce is designed to aggregate data based on specific criteria and provide subtotals and grand totals. It's useful for analyzing data trends, identifying patterns, and making data-driven decisions.

Why other options are incorrect:

B) A report that provides a flat list of records: This is a Tabular Report.

C) A report that tracks trends over time: While summary reports can be used to analyze trends, they are not specifically designed for time-based analysis. Trend reports are better suited for this purpose.

D) A report that shows data in a matrix format: This is a Matrix Report.

Additional considerations:

Summary reports can be grouped by multiple fields to provide hierarchical summaries.

They can be used in conjunction with charts to visualize data trends.

Summary reports are widely used in sales, marketing, and customer service departments.

Example: A sales manager wants to see the total sales revenue by region and product category. They can create a summary report with region and product category as grouping fields and sum the amount field to calculate the total sales for each combination.

79] Answer: D) Field

Explanation:

A Salesforce dashboard is a visual representation of key performance indicators (KPIs) and other important metrics. It's composed of various components that display data in a user-friendly format. These components include:

- Reports: Provide detailed data in tabular, summary, or matrix formats.
- Gauges: Display performance metrics using visual indicators.
- Charts: Present data graphically to reveal trends and patterns.

Fields are individual pieces of data within a record and are not standalone components on a dashboard. They are used within reports and charts to display specific information.

Therefore, Field is the correct answer as it's not a component of a dashboard itself but rather a data element used within dashboard components.

80] Answer: D) All of the above

Explanation:

To ensure that reports always reflect the most recent data, users can employ a combination of these methods:

A) By refreshing the report manually: This provides immediate access to the latest data but requires user intervention.

B) By scheduling the report to run at specific intervals: This automates the report generation process and ensures regular updates.

C) By using real-time data integration: If available, this provides the most up-to-date information continuously.

The optimal approach depends on the specific requirements of the report, the frequency of data changes, and the need for real-time insights.

Additional considerations:

131

Some report types might have inherent delays in data refresh, such as summary reports with large datasets.

Consider using dashboard components to display real-time or near-real-time data.

For critical reports, a combination of manual refresh and scheduling might be necessary.

By effectively utilizing these methods, users can maintain the accuracy and relevance of their reports.

81] Answer: D) All of the above

Explanation:

Salesforce offers multiple tools for automating business processes:

- Workflow Rules: These are used to automate simple actions based on record changes, such as sending email alerts or updating fields.
- Process Builder: A more advanced tool that allows for complex process automation, including multiple actions, conditions, and criteria.
- Approval Processes: Specifically designed to automate approval workflows, routing records for approval based on defined criteria.

While each tool has its strengths and use cases, they all contribute to automating repetitive tasks and streamlining business processes.

By understanding the capabilities of each option, you can choose the most appropriate tool for your specific automation needs.

82] B) 10

A single Workflow Rule can have a maximum of 10 time triggers. This limit is in place to optimize system performance and prevent excessive processing.

By understanding this limitation, you can effectively plan and design your workflow rules to meet your automation needs without exceeding the allowed number of time triggers.

83] Correct Answer:

A) Update the value of a field

Explanation:

A Workflow Rule is a powerful automation tool in Salesforce that allows you to perform specific actions based on certain criteria or events. One of its core functionalities is to update the value of a field. This means you can automatically change the content of a field when a particular condition is met.

Example:

A workflow rule can be set up to automatically populate the "Lead Source" field with "Website" if the "Origin" field equals "Website". This ensures data consistency and saves time for users.

Why Other Options are Incorrect:

B) Create a new record: This action is beyond the scope of a Workflow Rule. It requires more complex automation tools like Process Builder or Apex code.

C) Delete a record: Similar to creating a new record, deleting a record is not a function of Workflow Rules.

D) Export data: Workflow Rules are designed for internal data manipulation, not for exporting data to external systems.

Additional Considerations:

- Field Update Actions: While updating field values is the primary function, Workflow Rules can also be used to create tasks, send email alerts, and escalate records.
- Evaluation Criteria: Carefully define the conditions that trigger the Workflow Rule to ensure it functions as intended.
- Immediate vs. Time-Based Actions: Choose the appropriate timing for the field update based on your business requirements.
- Re-evaluation: Be aware of the potential for Workflow Rule re-evaluation if the updated field affects other Workflow Rules.

By understanding the capabilities and limitations of Workflow Rules, you can effectively automate your Salesforce processes and improve data quality.

84] Answer: B) Workflow Rules

Explanation:

Workflow Rules are the primary tool for automating actions based on specific criteria within Salesforce. One of the most common actions is sending email alerts.

You can define rules that specify when an email should be sent, to whom, and the content of the email based on changes to record fields, record creation, or other conditions.

Why other options are incorrect:

A) Email Templates: Email templates provide the content for emails but don't trigger the sending based on specific criteria.

C) Auto Response Rules: These are used to automatically send email responses to incoming emails, not based on internal Salesforce record changes.

D) Escalation Rules: These are specifically for escalating cases based on time-related criteria, not general email alerts.

By using Workflow Rules, you can create automated email notifications to keep users informed, streamline processes, and improve overall efficiency.

85] Answer: A) Automate approval of records based on criteria

Explanation:

Approval Processes in Salesforce are designed to streamline and control the approval workflow for records. They define the steps, approvers, and conditions for records to move through the approval process.

For example, you can set up an approval process for expense reports, contracts, or opportunity discounts, ensuring that records meet specific criteria before being finalized.

Why other options are incorrect:

B) Schedule data backups: Salesforce has built-in data backup mechanisms and doesn't rely on approval processes for this purpose.

C) Manage user permissions: User permissions are managed through profiles and permission sets, not approval processes.

D) Track sales performance: Salesforce offers reporting and dashboards for tracking sales performance. Approval processes are not directly related to this function.

By implementing approval processes, organizations can enforce compliance, reduce errors, and improve overall efficiency.

86] Answer: A) Mobile Layouts

Explanation:

Mobile Layouts are specifically designed to tailor the Salesforce user interface for mobile devices. They allow administrators to determine which fields and related lists are displayed on mobile screens.

By customizing mobile layouts, you can create a streamlined and efficient experience for users accessing Salesforce on their smartphones or tablets.

Why other options are incorrect:

B) Mobile Publisher: This is a tool for creating and managing mobile apps, but it doesn't focus on customizing the standard Salesforce mobile app.

C) Mobile Smart Actions: These are shortcuts for performing actions on mobile devices but don't impact the overall app layout.

D) Mobile Alerts: These are notifications sent to mobile devices but don't affect the app's appearance or functionality.

By using Mobile Layouts effectively, you can optimize the mobile experience for your users and increase productivity.

87] Answer: A) Access Salesforce data on mobile devices

Explanation:

The Salesforce mobile app is designed to provide users with on-the-go access to Salesforce data and functionalities. It allows users to view, create, edit, and update records, collaborate with colleagues, and perform various tasks related to their roles within the organization.

Why other options are incorrect:

B) Schedule data backups: Salesforce has its own data backup mechanisms, and the mobile app is not primarily for this purpose.

C) Manage user permissions: User permissions are managed through the Salesforce desktop interface using profiles and permission sets.

D) Track sales performance: While the mobile app can provide access to sales data, it's not specifically designed for comprehensive sales performance tracking.

The primary goal of the Salesforce mobile app is to enable users to stay connected to their Salesforce data and perform essential tasks from anywhere, anytime.

88] To optimize the Salesforce mobile app for users, administrators can customize various elements to tailor the experience to specific needs. This involves selecting the right tools to present information efficiently on smaller screens.

Correct Answer: D) All of the above

Compact Layouts: These layouts are specifically designed for smaller screens. They prioritize essential fields and display information in a condensed format, improving readability and navigation on mobile devices.

- List Views: Customizing list views allows you to determine which fields are displayed in mobile list views. This ensures that the most relevant information is readily available to users on the go.
- Search Layouts: By customizing search layouts, you can control the fields included in mobile search results. This helps users find the information they need quickly and efficiently.

Why Other Options are Incorrect:

A) Compact Layouts: While compact layouts are crucial for mobile optimization, they are not the only customizable element.

B) List Views: List views are essential for displaying records in a list format, but they are not the only factor in enhancing the mobile experience.

C) Search Layouts: Search layouts are important for efficient searching, but they do not encompass all aspects of mobile customization.

Additional Considerations:

Mobile-Optimized Page Layouts: While not explicitly mentioned in the options, creating mobile-optimized page layouts is also essential for a seamless user experience.

Testing: Thoroughly test the mobile app after making customizations to ensure optimal performance and user satisfaction.

User Feedback: Gather feedback from mobile users to identify areas for improvement and make necessary adjustments.

By carefully customizing compact layouts, list views, and search layouts, administrators can create a Salesforce mobile app that is efficient, user-friendly, and tailored to the specific needs of their organization.

89] The Mobile Navigation Menu is a crucial component of the Salesforce mobile app, designed to provide users with easy access to essential features and functionalities.

Correct Answer: A) Provide access to commonly used features

The primary purpose of the Mobile Navigation Menu is to offer users quick and convenient access to the features they use most frequently. By carefully selecting and arranging menu items, administrators can enhance user productivity and satisfaction.

Why Other Options are Incorrect:

B) Customize mobile app appearance: While the Mobile Navigation Menu is part of the mobile app's interface, its primary function is not to control the overall appearance.

C) Schedule mobile notifications: Mobile notifications are managed through different Salesforce settings and are not directly related to the navigation menu.

D) Manage mobile data sync: Mobile data sync is a system-level function and is not controlled through the navigation menu.

Additional Considerations:

Customizability: Administrators can customize the Mobile Navigation Menu to include specific objects, records, and actions based on user roles and needs.

Efficiency: A well-designed navigation menu can significantly improve user efficiency by reducing the number of taps required to access important features.

User Testing: Regularly test the Mobile Navigation Menu to ensure it meets user expectations and make adjustments as needed.

By effectively utilizing the Mobile Navigation Menu, administrators can create a mobile app experience that is both intuitive and efficient for users.

90] Salesforce offers multiple channels for users to receive notifications about updates within the platform. These notifications can be tailored to specific events or changes.

Correct Answer: D) All of the above

- Mobile Alerts: Salesforce Mobile Alerts allow users to receive push notifications for specific events like task reminders, record updates, or approval requests. These alerts are customizable and can be configured based on user preferences.

- Chatter Notifications: Users can subscribe to Chatter feeds and receive notifications for new posts, comments, or mentions. This keeps users updated on conversations and activities within their network.
- Salesforce1 Notifications: This refers to the broader category of notifications available in the Salesforce1 mobile app, including both Mobile Alerts and Chatter notifications, as well as other in-app notifications.

Why Other Options are Incorrect:

A), B), and C: While each option represents a valid way to receive notifications, Salesforce provides a comprehensive approach that includes all three methods to cater to different user preferences and notification requirements.

Additional Considerations:

Notification Preferences: Users can customize their notification settings to control the frequency and type of alerts they receive.

Mobile Device Settings: Ensure that users have enabled push notifications on their mobile devices for Salesforce to deliver alerts effectively.

Notification Channels: Salesforce offers various notification channels beyond mobile devices, including email and in-app notifications.

By leveraging all available notification options, users can stay informed about important updates within Salesforce, improving productivity and responsiveness.

91] AppExchange is Salesforce's online marketplace where businesses can find and implement pre-built applications, components, and services to extend the functionality of their Salesforce platform.

Correct Answer: A) A prebuilt app or component for Salesforce

AppExchange solutions are designed to address specific business needs and can be quickly deployed to enhance Salesforce's capabilities without the need for extensive development.

Why Other Options are Incorrect:

B) A tool for data integration: While some AppExchange solutions might offer data integration capabilities, it's not their primary purpose.

C) A reporting tool: While there are reporting tools available on AppExchange, it's again, not the core function of the platform.

D) A data backup service: Data backup is a specific functionality and while there might be solutions for this on AppExchange, it's not the overall purpose.

Additional Considerations:

Customization: Many AppExchange solutions offer customization options to fit specific business requirements.

Variety: The AppExchange marketplace offers a wide range of solutions for various industries and departments.

Cost: AppExchange solutions can be free, paid, or offered on a subscription basis.

By leveraging AppExchange, businesses can accelerate their Salesforce implementation and gain a competitive advantage by accessing innovative solutions.

92] Once a package is installed from AppExchange, administrators have the responsibility to manage its components, licenses, and overall lifecycle within their Salesforce org.

Correct Answer: A) Using the Installed Packages page

The Installed Packages page is the centralized location within Salesforce where administrators can view, manage, and take actions on all installed packages. *This includes:*

- Viewing package details
- Assigning licenses to users
- Upgrading packages (if available)
- Uninstalling packages

Why Other Options are Incorrect:

B) Through the AppExchange website: While you can find and install packages on the AppExchange website, managing them after installation is done within your Salesforce org.

C) By contacting Salesforce support: While Salesforce support can assist with general inquiries, managing installed packages is a standard administrative task.

D) Using the Data Import Wizard: The Data Import Wizard is used for importing data into Salesforce, not for managing packages.

Additional Considerations:

Package Licenses: Carefully manage package licenses to ensure optimal utilization and avoid unnecessary costs.

Package Upgrades: Regularly check for package updates to benefit from new features and bug fixes.

Package Dependencies: Be aware of any dependencies between installed packages to avoid conflicts during upgrades or uninstallation.

By effectively managing installed packages, administrators can optimize the value of AppExchange solutions and maintain the overall health of their Salesforce org.

93. AppExchange solutions come in different packaging formats, each with varying levels of customization allowed for the installing organization.

Correct Answer: A) Managed Packages

Managed Packages: These are pre-built applications that are tightly controlled by the package developer. The installing organization cannot modify the package's code or components. This ensures consistency and prevents potential issues with the package's functionality.

Why Other Options are Incorrect:

- Unmanaged Packages: These packages allow for full customization by the installing organization. They are often used for sharing components within an organization or with trusted partners.
- Custom Apps: While these are not AppExchange solutions, they are customizable by the organization that creates them.
- Visual force Pages: These are components that can be modified within an organization, regardless of whether they are part of a managed or unmanaged package.

Additional Considerations:

Managed Package Licensing: Managed packages are typically licensed, and the terms of the license dictate the level of access and customization allowed.

AppExchange Evaluation: Carefully evaluate the level of customization needed before choosing between managed and unmanaged packages.

Understanding the differences between managed and unmanaged packages is crucial for selecting the right AppExchange solution and managing it effectively within an organization.

94] AppExchange partners play a vital role in expanding the capabilities of the Salesforce platform. They contribute to the ecosystem by offering a variety of products and services.

Correct Answer: D) All of the above

AppExchange partners encompass a diverse range of roles within the Salesforce ecosystem:

Provide support and services: Partners offer implementation, customization, training, and ongoing support for Salesforce solutions.

Develop and distribute apps: They create and distribute innovative applications to address specific business needs on the AppExchange marketplace.

Offer training and consulting: Partners provide expertise in Salesforce best practices, configuration, and process improvement.

Why Other Options are Incorrect:

Given the breadth of activities undertaken by AppExchange partners, none of the individual options fully encapsulate their contributions to the ecosystem.

Additional Considerations:

Partner Tiers: Salesforce offers different partner tiers based on the level of commitment and expertise.

Partner Specialization: Partners often specialize in specific industries or Salesforce modules, offering in-depth knowledge.

Customer Value: AppExchange partners help customers maximize their investment in Salesforce by providing tailored solutions and support.

By collaborating with AppExchange partners, organizations can accelerate their Salesforce adoption, enhance productivity, and achieve their business goals more effectively.

95] Evaluating AppExchange solutions is crucial to selecting the right fit for your organization. A thorough evaluation process helps mitigate risks and ensures the solution meets your specific requirements.

Correct Answer: D) All of the above

A comprehensive evaluation involves a combination of these practices:

Reading reviews and ratings: User feedback provides valuable insights into the solution's strengths, weaknesses, and overall performance.

Checking for certifications: Salesforce certifications indicate that the solution meets specific quality standards and compatibility requirements.

Testing in a sandbox environment: This allows you to assess the solution's functionality, performance, and impact on your Salesforce org without affecting production data.

Additional Considerations:

- Define Your Requirements: Clearly outline your business needs and the specific functionalities you expect from the AppExchange solution.
- Consider Cost: Evaluate the pricing model (licensing, subscription, etc.) and its alignment with your budget.
- Security and Compliance: Verify that the solution meets your organization's security and compliance standards.
- Vendor Support: Assess the vendor's reputation, support options, and responsiveness.

By following these best practices, you can increase the likelihood of selecting an AppExchange solution that delivers value and meets your organization's goals.

96] Service Level Agreements (SLAs) define the expected level of service between a service provider and a customer. Salesforce provides several features to help organizations manage and track SLAs effectively.

Correct Answer: B) Entitlements

Entitlements are the core component for managing SLAs in Salesforce. They define the specific terms of service for a customer, including:

- SLA metrics (response time, resolution time, etc.)
- Entitlement terms (duration, quantity)
- Products or services covered

By associating cases with entitlements, Salesforce can automatically calculate SLA metrics and generate alerts when SLAs are at risk or breached.

Why Other Options are Incorrect:

- Milestones: While milestones can be used to track specific points in a process, they are not specifically designed for SLA tracking.
- Case Escalations: Case escalations are triggered when a case reaches a certain severity level or exceeds SLA thresholds, but they don't track the overall SLA progress.
- Service Contracts: Service contracts are legal agreements outlining the terms of service, but they don't provide the detailed tracking capabilities of entitlements.

Additional Considerations:

Entitlement Processes: These can be used to automate actions based on entitlement criteria, such as creating tasks or escalating cases.

SLA Metrics: Salesforce provides standard SLA metrics, but you can also create custom metrics to meet specific business requirements.

Reporting: Entitlement data can be used to generate reports and dashboards to monitor SLA performance and identify areas for improvement.

By effectively utilizing entitlements, organizations can ensure adherence to SLAs, improve customer satisfaction, and optimize their service delivery processes.

97] Answer: A) Assign multiple users to a case

Explanation:

The Case Team feature in Salesforce enables you to assign multiple users to a single case. This is particularly useful for cases that require the involvement of multiple departments or individuals to resolve. Each team member can be assigned a specific role, providing clear responsibilities and improving collaboration.

Why other options are incorrect:

B) Track case metrics: Case metrics are tracked using reports and dashboards, not the Case Team feature.

C) Automate case routing: Case routing is typically handled through assignment rules and automation rules.

D) Merge duplicate cases: There is a specific merge duplicate cases function within Salesforce, distinct from Case Teams.

By utilizing Case Teams, organizations can enhance case management efficiency, improve collaboration, and ensure that cases are handled effectively by the appropriate team members.

98] Answer: A) Cases

Explanation:

The Service Console is specifically designed to streamline case management processes for customer service agents. It provides a centralized workspace for handling customer inquiries, issues, and requests efficiently.

Why other options are incorrect:

B) Opportunities, C) Leads, D) Campaigns: While these objects are essential parts of Salesforce, they are primarily related to sales and marketing functions, not customer service. The Service Console focuses on case management.

By using the Service Console, agents can efficiently create, update, and resolve cases, improving customer satisfaction and overall service efficiency.

99] Answer: A) By Categories

Explanation:

Data Categories are the primary method for organizing knowledge articles in Salesforce Knowledge. They allow you to create a hierarchical structure for categorizing articles based on specific topics, products, or subject areas. This makes it easier for users to find relevant information quickly.

Why other options are incorrect:

B) By Data Type: Data types refer to the fields used to store information within an article, not for organizing the articles themselves.

C) By User Role: While you can control access to knowledge articles based on user roles, this doesn't organize the articles themselves.

D) By Custom Fields: Custom fields can be added to knowledge articles for additional information, but they are not used for primary organization.

By effectively utilizing data categories, you can create a well-structured knowledge base that improves search results and enhances user experience.

100] Answer: B) Knowledge Base

Explanation:

A Knowledge Base is a centralized repository of information that customers can access to find answers to their questions independently. It typically contains articles, FAQs, and other self-help resources. By providing customers with a self-service option, organizations can reduce case volume and improve customer satisfaction.

Why other options are incorrect:

A) Self-Service Portal: While a self-service portal can host a knowledge base, it's not the knowledge repository itself.

C) Case Management: Case management is primarily used by support agents to manage customer issues.

D) Chatter: Chatter is a social collaboration tool and not designed for self-service knowledge sharing.

By implementing a robust knowledge base, businesses can empower customers to find solutions quickly and efficiently, leading to improved customer experience and reduced support costs.

101] Answer: B) Task Manager

Explanation:

The Task Manager in Salesforce is specifically designed for creating, assigning, and managing tasks. It allows users to:

- Create new tasks
- Assign tasks to specific users or groups
- Set due dates and reminders
- Prioritize tasks
- Track task completion

Why other options are incorrect:

A) Activity Timeline: While it displays tasks, it's primarily for viewing and managing activities related to records.

C) Calendar: Used for scheduling events and appointments, not for assigning tasks.

D) Chatter: A social collaboration tool, not task management focused.

By effectively using the Task Manager, teams can improve task delegation, accountability, and overall productivity.

102] Answer: A) Provide a historical view of activities related to a record

Explanation:

The Activity Timeline in Salesforce is a centralized location where you can view all past, present, and future activities associated with a specific record. This includes tasks, events, emails, calls, and other relevant interactions.

Why it's the correct answer:

- Historical perspective: The Activity Timeline offers a chronological view of all interactions related to a record, providing valuable insights into the record's history.
- Centralized location: All activities are consolidated in one place, making it easy to access and analyze information.
- Improved collaboration: Teams can easily see what actions have been taken, who took them, and when, fostering better collaboration.

Why other options are incorrect:

B) Schedule future tasks and events: While you can view upcoming tasks and events in the Activity Timeline, its primary purpose is to provide a historical view. Scheduling is typically done through the calendar or task management features.

C) Track sales opportunities: The Activity Timeline is used for tracking activities related to various records, including opportunities, but it's not specifically designed for opportunity tracking.

D) Manage user permissions: User permissions are managed in the Security Controls section of Salesforce, not the Activity Timeline.

Additional Considerations:

The Activity Timeline can be customized to display different types of activities and information.

It integrates with other Salesforce features like Einstein Activity Capture to automatically log activities.

The Activity Timeline is a valuable tool for sales reps, customer service agents, and other users who need to understand the history of a record.

By understanding the Activity Timeline, Salesforce administrators can effectively configure it to meet the needs of their organization and improve user productivity.

146

103] Answer: D) All of the above

Explanation:

All of the options provided are effective ways to stay informed about updates in a Chatter feed.

A) By setting up email notifications: Users can configure email notifications for specific types of Chatter updates, ensuring they receive timely alerts.

B) By following relevant records and groups: Following records and groups allows users to see updates related to their areas of interest directly in their Chatter feed.

C) By creating custom feeds: Users can create personalized feeds to focus on specific topics or content, helping them stay organized and informed.

By combining these methods, users can create a comprehensive approach to staying up-to-date with important information within Salesforce Chatter.

104] Answer: A) A feature to survey opinions

Explanation:

A Chatter Poll is a tool within Salesforce that allows users to gather feedback and opinions from colleagues by creating quick and easy surveys. It's a collaborative feature that encourages participation and decision-making within a group.

Why it's the correct answer:

Opinion gathering: Chatter Polls are designed specifically for collecting diverse perspectives on a particular topic.

Quick and easy: Creating and participating in polls is straightforward, making it a convenient way to gather input.

Collaborative: Polls foster engagement and discussion among team members.

Why other options are incorrect:

B) A tool to assign tasks: Task assignment is typically handled through other Salesforce features like Workflows or Queues.

C) A way to schedule events: Event scheduling is done through the Salesforce Calendar or Event management tools.

D) A data backup service: Data backup is a separate function managed by Salesforce's data management tools.

Additional Considerations:

Chatter Polls can be used for various purposes, such as gathering feedback on product ideas, project planning, or team preferences.

Poll results can be viewed and analyzed to inform decision-making.

Chatter Polls can be shared with specific groups or with the entire organization.

By understanding Chatter Polls, Salesforce administrators can help users leverage this tool to improve collaboration and decision-making within their teams.

105] Answer: A) Chatter Files

Explanation:

Chatter Files is the Salesforce feature specifically designed for creating, sharing, and collaborating on documents within the platform. It provides a centralized location for storing, accessing, and managing files related to different records and projects.

Why it's the correct answer:

Centralized storage: Chatter Files offers a unified place to store various document types.

Sharing capabilities: Users can easily share files with colleagues, teams, or external parties.

Collaboration: The platform allows multiple users to work on a document simultaneously and track changes.

Integration with records: Files can be associated with specific Salesforce records, improving organization and accessibility.

Why other options are incorrect:

B) Document Manager: While this might sound like a suitable option, Salesforce doesn't have a standalone feature called Document Manager.

C) File Sharing: This is too general a term and doesn't accurately reflect the specific functionality provided by Chatter Files.

D) Content Library: Content Libraries are typically used for storing and managing marketing assets, not general document collaboration.

Additional Considerations:

Chatter Files integrates with other Salesforce features like Chatter feeds for discussions around documents.

Administrators can control file sharing permissions and access levels to protect sensitive information.

Users can leverage version control to track changes and restore previous versions of documents.

By understanding Chatter Files, Salesforce administrators can effectively configure and utilize this feature to enhance document management and collaboration within their organization.

106] Answer: B) Duplicate Rules

Explanation:

Duplicate Rules are specifically designed to identify and prevent the creation of duplicate records in Salesforce. They define the criteria for determining when two records are considered duplicates and specify the actions to be taken when a potential duplicate is found.

Why it's the correct answer:

Duplicate identification: Duplicate Rules define matching criteria based on specific fields (e.g., email address, account name) to identify potential duplicates.

Preventive actions: You can configure Duplicate Rules to block the creation of duplicates, display a warning, or allow users to merge duplicates.

Customization: Duplicate Rules can be tailored to specific objects and business requirements.

Why other options are incorrect:

A) Validation Rules: While Validation Rules can prevent data entry errors, they are not specifically designed to identify duplicates.

C) Workflow Rules: Workflow Rules automate actions based on record changes, but they don't focus on duplicate prevention.

D) Escalation Rules: Escalation Rules are used to route records through approval processes, unrelated to duplicate management.

Additional Considerations:

Duplicate Rules work in conjunction with Matching Rules which define the exact logic for comparing records.

Salesforce provides standard Duplicate Rules for Accounts, Contacts, and Leads, but you can create custom rules for other objects.

Effective duplicate prevention requires careful consideration of matching criteria and appropriate actions.

By implementing Duplicate Rules, Salesforce administrators can significantly reduce the occurrence of duplicate records, improving data quality and efficiency.

107] Answer: B) A way to define the relationships and fields available for reporting

Explanation:

A Custom Report Type in Salesforce is essentially a blueprint that defines the structure of a report. It specifies which objects and their related fields should be included in the report. By creating custom report types, you can tailor the reporting capabilities to your specific business needs.

Why it's the correct answer:

Defines relationships: Custom report types establish the connections between different objects, allowing you to report on data from multiple sources.

Determines available fields: They specify which fields from the included objects will be accessible in the report.

Flexibility: Custom report types provide the foundation for creating various report formats to suit different reporting requirements.

Why other options are incorrect:

A) A report format that can be customized: While you can customize the format of a report, the custom report type defines the underlying data structure.

C) A data export tool: Data export is a separate function in Salesforce, unrelated to custom report types.

D) A data import tool: Data import tools are used to bring data into Salesforce, not for reporting purposes.

Additional Considerations:

Custom report types are essential for creating complex reports that involve multiple objects and fields.

They can be used to generate standard, summary, and matrix reports.

Salesforce provides standard report types for common reporting needs, but custom report types offer greater flexibility.

By understanding custom report types, Salesforce administrators can create powerful and informative reports to support decision-making within the organization.

108] Answer: D) Using Workflow Rules

Explanation:

While there are other methods to delete data in Salesforce, Workflow Rules provide the most effective and automated way to delete obsolete data based on specific criteria.

Why it's the correct answer:

- Automation: Workflow Rules can be set up to automatically trigger actions based on specific record conditions.
- Criteria-based deletion: You can define criteria to identify records that meet the "obsolete" status, such as a specific date field or record status.
- Flexible actions: Workflow Rules can initiate the deletion of records when the specified criteria are met.

Why other options are incorrect:

A) Using Data Export Service: This service is used to export data, not delete it.

B) Using Data Loader: Data Loader is a bulk data import/export tool, not designed for automated deletion.

C) Using Mass Delete Records: While this option allows you to delete multiple records at once, it's a manual process and doesn't provide automation.

Additional Considerations:

Careful planning: It's crucial to define clear criteria for determining which data is considered obsolete.

Data retention policies: Ensure compliance with data retention requirements before implementing deletion rules.

Testing: Thoroughly test the workflow rule to avoid accidental data loss.

Backup: Maintain regular data backups as an additional safety measure.

By effectively using Workflow Rules, Salesforce administrators can maintain data quality and storage efficiency by automatically removing obsolete information.

109] Answer: B) Duplicate Management

Explanation:

Duplicate Management is the specific Salesforce feature designed to address the issue of duplicate records. It includes tools to identify, prevent, and merge duplicate records, helping to maintain data accuracy and consistency.

Why it's the correct answer:

Duplicate identification: Duplicate Management allows you to define rules to identify potential duplicates based on specific criteria.

Duplicate prevention: You can set up actions to prevent the creation of new duplicate records.

Duplicate merging: The feature provides tools to merge duplicate records into a single, accurate record.

Why other options are incorrect:

A) Data Cleansing: While related to data quality, data cleansing typically involves correcting existing data errors rather than preventing duplicates.

C) Data Quality Rules: These rules are used to enforce data standards and consistency, but they don't specifically address duplicate records.

D) Data Merging: This is a general term and doesn't accurately reflect the specific functionality provided by Duplicate Management.

Additional Considerations:

Duplicate Management works in conjunction with Matching Rules and Duplicate Rules to define how duplicates are identified and handled.

Effective duplicate management is crucial for maintaining data integrity and improving report accuracy.

Regular review and maintenance of duplicate management settings are essential.

By utilizing Duplicate Management, Salesforce administrators can significantly enhance data quality and improve overall Salesforce performance.

110] Answer: D) No limit

Explanation:

The Data Export Service in Salesforce is designed to handle large-scale data exports without imposing a strict record limit. It's capable of exporting millions of records, making it suitable for various data migration and analysis tasks.

Why it's the correct answer:

Large-scale exports: The Data Export Service is specifically built to handle massive data sets efficiently.

No artificial limits: Salesforce doesn't impose a hard cap on the number of records that can be exported.

Flexible export options: You can export data in various formats (CSV, ZIP) and choose specific objects and fields.

Why other options are incorrect:

The provided options (50,000, 100,000, 500,000) are significantly lower than the actual export capacity of the Data Export Service.

Additional Considerations:

While there's no strict record limit, export performance might be affected by data volume and complexity.

Salesforce recommends using the Data Export Service for large data sets rather than manual methods or other export tools.

Consider data governance policies and export limitations imposed by your organization.

By understanding the capabilities of the Data Export Service, Salesforce administrators can effectively manage large-scale data extraction and transfer processes.

111] Answer: B) Dynamic Dashboards

Explanation:

Dynamic Dashboards are the core tool for combining multiple reports into a single, interactive view in Salesforce. They provide a visual representation of key performance indicators (KPIs) and data trends, allowing users to easily analyze and understand information.

Why it's the correct answer:

Multiple report display: Dashboards can incorporate various report types (summary, matrix, tabular) to present a comprehensive overview.

Customization: Users can arrange and resize dashboard components to create a customized layout.

Interactivity: Dashboards often include interactive elements like filters and drill-down capabilities.

Why other options are incorrect:

A) Report Snapshots: These are static images of reports, not designed for combining multiple reports on a single page.

C) Report Charts: Charts are visual representations of data within a single report, not a tool for combining reports.

D) Dashboard Components: These are individual elements within a dashboard (like charts, tables, metrics), not the dashboard itself.

Additional Considerations:

Dashboards can be shared with other users or made public for broader access.

They are often used for sales performance tracking, customer support metrics, and other business-critical information.

Effective dashboard design is essential for clear communication and data-driven decision-making.

By leveraging Dynamic Dashboards, Salesforce users can gain valuable insights from their data and make informed decisions.

112] Answer: A) Highlight cells based on criteria

Explanation:

Conditional Highlighting is a feature in Salesforce reports that allows you to visually emphasize specific data points by applying colors to cells based on predefined conditions. This helps users quickly identify trends, outliers, or critical information within the report.

Why it's the correct answer:

Visual emphasis: Conditional highlighting uses color to draw attention to specific data points.

Data-driven formatting: The highlighting is based on defined criteria, such as value ranges or specific conditions.

Improved readability: It enhances report clarity and understanding.

Why other options are incorrect:

B) Schedule report refreshes: This is the function of report subscriptions.

C) Customize report filters: Report filters are used to modify the data displayed in a report.

D) Share reports with other users: Reports can be shared using sharing settings and permissions.

Additional Considerations:

Conditional highlighting can be applied to summary and matrix reports.

Multiple highlighting rules can be created for a single report.

Effective use of conditional highlighting requires careful consideration of color choices and criteria.

By using conditional highlighting, Salesforce users can create more informative and visually appealing reports.

113] Answer: A) Summary Report

Explanation:

A Summary Report in Salesforce is the most suitable option for visualizing trends over time. It allows you to group data by specific fields (like date, month, or quarter) and calculate summary values (like sum, average, count) for each group. This provides a clear picture of how data changes over time.

Why it's the correct answer:

Time-based grouping: You can easily group data by time periods to analyze trends.

Summary calculations: Summary reports provide calculations like sum, average, and count to quantify changes.

Charting capabilities: You can create various chart types (line, bar, pie) to visually represent the data.

Why other options are incorrect:

B) Tabular Report: While useful for displaying data in a table format, it doesn't provide a visual representation of trends.

C) Matrix Report: Matrix reports are better suited for comparing data across multiple dimensions, not for visualizing trends over time.

D) Analytical Snapshot: This is not a standard report type in Salesforce.

By utilizing Summary Reports with appropriate grouping and charting, Salesforce users can effectively analyze and communicate data trends.

114] Answer: A) Categorize report records without creating a formula or custom field

Explanation:

A Bucket Field in Salesforce is a powerful tool that allows you to categorize data within a report without the need to create a custom formula field or modify the underlying object. It provides a flexible way to group records based on specific criteria, enhancing data analysis and reporting capabilities.

Why it's the correct answer:

Categorization without custom fields: Bucket fields offer a quick and efficient way to group data without altering the object structure.

Enhanced reporting: By creating custom categories, you can analyze data in new and meaningful ways.

Improved data visualization: Buckets can be used to create more informative charts and graphs.

Why other options are incorrect:

B) Aggregate data from multiple fields: This is typically done using summary formulas or roll-up summaries.

C) Create cross-object summaries: Cross-object summaries involve relationships between objects and are not related to bucket fields.

D) Set up report filters: Filters are used to narrow down the data displayed in a report, not to categorize it.

Additional Considerations:

Bucket fields can be used in summary, tabular, and matrix reports.

You can define multiple buckets for a single field.

Bucket fields can be combined with other report features to create complex analyses.

By understanding and effectively using bucket fields, Salesforce administrators and users can improve data analysis and reporting efficiency.

115] Answer: A) Using Field-Level Security

Explanation:

Field-Level Security (FLS) is the most effective way to protect sensitive data from being exposed in shared reports. By controlling access to specific fields at the user or role level, you can prevent unauthorized individuals from viewing sensitive information.

Why it's the correct answer:

Granular control: FLS allows you to precisely determine which users can view specific fields.

Data protection: By restricting access to sensitive fields, you safeguard confidential information.

Compliance: FLS helps organizations comply with data privacy regulations.

Why other options are incorrect:

B) By creating private reports: While creating private reports limits report visibility, it doesn't prevent sensitive data from being included if the user has access to the underlying data.

C) By applying report filters: Report filters can exclude certain records from a report, but they don't restrict access to specific fields.

D) By using report folders: Report folders organize reports but don't control data visibility.

Additional Considerations:

Combine FLS with other security measures like role hierarchies and data masking for comprehensive protection.

Regularly review and update FLS settings to reflect changes in data sensitivity and user roles.

Consider using data loss prevention (DLP) policies to further safeguard sensitive information.

By implementing robust FLS, organizations can protect sensitive data while maintaining the necessary access for authorized users.

116] Answer: B) Approval Processes

Explanation:

Approval Processes are specifically designed to create and manage multi-step approval workflows within Salesforce. They provide the flexibility to define the sequence of approvals, assign approvers, and handle various approval scenarios.

Why it's the correct answer:

Approval steps: You can define multiple approval steps with specific criteria and approvers.

Approval routing: Approval processes can route records through different approval paths based on specific conditions.

Notifications: You can configure email notifications for approval requests and decisions.

Why other options are incorrect:

A) Workflow Rules: While workflow rules can automate actions based on record changes, they are not specifically designed for complex approval processes.

C) Process Builder: Process Builder is a more general automation tool, not tailored for approval workflows.

D) Validation Rules: Validation rules are used to enforce data integrity, not to manage approval processes.

Additional Considerations:

Approval processes can be used for various record types, such as opportunities, contracts, and custom objects.

You can set up parallel, sequential, or complex approval paths based on your business requirements.

Approval processes can be combined with other automation tools like workflow rules and process builder for more advanced scenarios.

By effectively using approval processes, organizations can streamline their approval workflows, reduce errors, and improve efficiency.

117] Answer: A) An action that is triggered at a specific time

Explanation:

A Time-Dependent Workflow Action in Salesforce is an automated action that is executed at a predetermined point in time relative to a specific date on a record. This allows you to schedule tasks, send reminders, or update records based on a defined time frame.

Why it's the correct answer:

Time-based triggering: The action is initiated at a specific time interval before or after a designated date field on the record.

Scheduled automation: You can set up actions to occur days or hours before or after a specific event.

Flexibility: Time-dependent actions offer a high degree of customization for automated processes.

Why other options are incorrect:

B) An action that is triggered based on a field value: This describes a standard workflow rule.

C) An action that runs in realtime: This is not specific to time-dependent workflow actions.

D) An action that is scheduled to run periodically: This is more akin to scheduled jobs or batch processes.

Additional Considerations:

Time-dependent actions are often used for reminders, escalations, or follow-up tasks.

You can define multiple time-dependent actions for a single workflow rule.

Careful planning is essential to ensure that time-dependent actions align with your business processes.

By effectively using time-dependent workflow actions, Salesforce administrators can automate tasks and improve efficiency.

118] Answer: B) Process Builder

Explanation:

Process Builder is a powerful tool in Salesforce that enables users to create automated processes with a visual, drag-and-drop interface. It allows you to define complex business logic, create records, update fields, send emails, and more based on specific criteria.

Why it's the correct answer:

Visual interface: Process Builder provides a user-friendly interface for building automation without requiring coding.

Complex process automation: It can handle intricate business processes involving multiple steps and decisions.

Flexibility: Process Builder offers various actions and conditions to accommodate diverse automation needs.

Why other options are incorrect:

A) Workflow Rules: While useful for simple automations, workflow rules are limited in complexity compared to Process Builder.

C) Approval Processes: Specifically designed for approval workflows, Approval Processes are not as versatile as Process Builder for general automation.

D) Validation Rules: Validation Rules are used to enforce data integrity and prevent invalid data entry, not for automation.

Additional Considerations:

Process Builder can be used to automate a wide range of business processes, such as lead-to-opportunity conversions, case management, and approval workflows.

It can be combined with other automation tools like Workflow Rules and Approval Processes for more comprehensive solutions.

Effective use of Process Builder requires careful planning and testing to ensure desired outcomes.

By leveraging Process Builder, Salesforce administrators can streamline operations, improve efficiency, and enhance user experience.

119] A Workflow Rule is an automation tool in Salesforce that executes a set of actions when specific criteria are met. Actions can include sending emails, updating fields, creating tasks, and more.

Answer: B) 10

Explanation:

By default, a single Workflow Rule can perform a maximum of 10 actions. However, it's essential to note that this limit can be increased up to 25 by contacting Salesforce Support.

Why other options are incorrect:

A) 5: This number is significantly lower than the default limit.

C) 20: While closer to the default, it's still below the actual limit.

D) Unlimited: This is incorrect as Salesforce imposes limits to ensure system performance and stability.

Additional Considerations:

Increasing the limit: If you require more than 10 actions, you can request an increase from Salesforce Support. However, be aware that excessive actions can impact system performance.

Alternatives to Workflow Rules: For complex automation scenarios, consider using Process Builder or Flow as they offer greater flexibility and scalability.

Best practices: To optimize Workflow Rule performance, limit the number of actions and conditions to avoid unnecessary processing.

Example: Imagine a Workflow Rule that triggers when an Opportunity stage changes to "Closed Won". You might have 10 actions set up, such as sending a congratulatory email to the sales rep, creating a task to follow up with the customer, updating related records, and more.

By understanding these limitations and best practices, you can effectively utilize Workflow Rules to automate your business processes within Salesforce.

120] Salesforce offers several tools to automate record updates based on specific conditions. Each tool has its strengths and use cases.

Answer: B) Using Workflow Rules

Explanation:

Workflow Rules are specifically designed to perform actions (including record updates) when certain criteria are met. They are a powerful and straightforward tool for automating routine tasks.

Why other options are incorrect:

A) Validation Rules: These are used to enforce data integrity by preventing invalid data from being saved. They don't automatically update records.

C) Approval Processes: These are used to route records through a predefined approval process, not for automatic updates based on criteria.

D) Process Builder: While Process Builder is a more advanced automation tool, it's overkill for simple record updates based on criteria. Workflow Rules are more suitable for this purpose.

Additional Considerations:

Workflow Rule Criteria: You can define complex conditions using fields, formulas, and related records to trigger the rule.

Workflow Rule Actions: Besides updating records, Workflow Rules can also send emails, create tasks, and more.

Performance: Be mindful of the number of Workflow Rules and actions to avoid performance issues.

Example: Imagine you want to automatically update the "Stage" field on an Opportunity to "Closed Won" when the "Amount" reaches $100,000. A Workflow Rule with the appropriate criteria and update action would accomplish this.

By understanding the capabilities of Workflow Rules, you can significantly streamline your Salesforce processes and improve data accuracy.

121] Answer: B) Publish custom mobile apps

Explanation:

Mobile Publisher is a tool within Salesforce that empowers users to create and distribute customized mobile apps without requiring extensive coding knowledge. It allows businesses to tailor the Salesforce mobile experience to their specific needs and branding.

Why other options are incorrect:

A) Customize the mobile app interface: While Mobile Publisher does allow for customization, it goes beyond just the interface. It enables the creation of entirely new mobile apps.

C) Schedule mobile notifications: Salesforce offers other tools like Einstein Bots and Marketing Cloud for scheduling mobile notifications.

D) Sync mobile data with Salesforce: Salesforce already provides robust data synchronization capabilities between the mobile app and the Salesforce platform. Mobile Publisher's focus is on app creation and customization.

Additional Considerations:

Key Features: Mobile Publisher includes features like app branding, configuration, deployment, and management.

App Distribution: Once created, apps can be distributed through app stores or internally within the organization.

Use Cases: Common use cases include field service, sales, and customer support.

Example: A company wants to create a mobile app for its sales team that focuses on lead management and opportunity tracking. Using Mobile Publisher, they can customize the app's look and feel, select the relevant Salesforce data, and deploy the app to their sales reps.

By leveraging Mobile Publisher, organizations can enhance user experience, increase productivity, and strengthen their mobile strategy.

122] Answer: B) Salesforce1 Notifications

Explanation:

Salesforce1 Notifications are specifically designed to deliver real-time alerts and updates to users' mobile devices. They are essential for keeping users informed about critical events, such as new leads, case escalations, or record updates.

Why other options are incorrect:

A) Mobile Alerts: This is a general term that doesn't specifically refer to push notifications.

C) Chatter Notifications: While Chatter is used for internal communication, it doesn't inherently provide push notifications to mobile devices.

D) Workflow Alerts: Workflow Alerts are primarily used for email notifications, not push notifications.

Additional Considerations:

Customization: Salesforce1 Notifications can be customized with specific content and actions.

Triggers: You can define criteria to determine when notifications should be sent.

User Preferences: Users can control their notification settings.

Example: A sales rep receives a push notification when a new lead is assigned to them, allowing them to quickly follow up and increase the chance of conversion.

By effectively utilizing Salesforce1 Notifications, organizations can improve responsiveness, productivity, and overall user experience.

123] Answer: C) Mobile Layout

Explanation:

Mobile Layout is specifically designed to optimize the user experience on mobile devices. It allows administrators to tailor the layout, fields, and sections displayed on mobile screens for efficient data access and input.

Why Other Options Are Incorrect:

Compact Layout provides a summarized view of a record, but it's not exclusive to mobile devices. It can be used on both desktop and mobile.

Page Layout is the primary layout for a record, determining the overall structure of fields and sections. It can be customized for desktop and mobile, but it's not specifically optimized for mobile.

Record Layout is not a standard Salesforce term.

Additional Considerations:

When creating a Mobile Layout, consider the screen size limitations of mobile devices.

Prioritize essential fields and information for quick access.

Use clear and concise labels.

Test the layout on different mobile devices to ensure optimal performance.

By carefully designing Mobile Layouts, administrators can enhance user productivity and satisfaction on Salesforce mobile apps.

124] Answer: A) By using the Salesforce mobile app

Explanation:

The Salesforce mobile app is specifically designed to provide on-the-go access to Salesforce data. It offers a user-friendly interface, optimized for smaller screens, and provides features tailored for mobile use.

Why Other Options Are Incorrect:

Using a web browser is possible, but it's not ideal for mobile devices due to performance and user experience limitations.

Mobile emulators are used for development purposes, not for end-user access.

Desktop sync tools are for synchronizing data between desktop and Salesforce, not for direct mobile access.

Additional Considerations:

Salesforce offers both native mobile apps and a mobile browser experience.

The features available in the mobile app might be slightly different from the desktop version.

Administrators can customize the mobile experience using Mobile Layouts.

By utilizing the Salesforce mobile app, users can efficiently access and manage Salesforce data from anywhere, anytime.

125] Answer: C) Provide quick actions for common tasks

Explanation:

Mobile Smart Actions offer a streamlined way to perform frequent tasks directly from the Salesforce mobile app. They are preconfigured actions that can be accessed quickly, improving user efficiency and productivity.

Why Other Options Are Incorrect:

Automate repetitive tasks: While Mobile Smart Actions can help with repetitive tasks, their primary purpose is to provide quick access to actions, not full automation.

Enable voice commands: Salesforce does offer voice commands through integration with voice assistants, but this is a separate feature and not related to Mobile Smart Actions.

Sync data between mobile and desktop: Data synchronization is a core functionality of the Salesforce mobile app, but Mobile Smart Actions focus on user actions, not data management.

Additional Considerations:

Mobile Smart Actions can be customized to meet specific business needs.

They can be used to create new records, edit existing records, or initiate workflows.

By strategically implementing Mobile Smart Actions, administrators can significantly enhance the mobile user experience.

126] Answer: A) An app that can be updated by the provider

Explanation:

A Managed Package on AppExchange is a pre-built application developed by a third-party provider. The key characteristic of a managed package is that the provider maintains control over the package and can release updates, bug fixes, and new features. Users who install the package benefit from these updates without needing to make any changes themselves.

Why Other Options Are Incorrect:

An app that cannot be modified by the user: While users cannot modify the core components of a managed package, they can often configure settings and customize the package to fit their specific needs.

An app that includes prebuilt components: This is true, but it doesn't capture the essence of a managed package's update and maintenance capabilities.

An app that integrates with external systems: While many managed packages offer integrations, this is not a defining characteristic.

Additional Considerations:

166

Managed packages offer a secure and efficient way to deploy custom applications across multiple Salesforce organizations.

Providers can monetize their packages through licensing and subscription models.

Users should carefully review the terms and conditions of a managed package before installation.

By understanding the nature of managed packages, administrators can effectively evaluate and implement third-party solutions to enhance their Salesforce organization's capabilities.

127] Answer: D) All of the above

Explanation:

AppExchange offers multiple ways to discover solutions tailored to specific business needs:

Browsing categories: AppExchange is organized into categories like Sales, Service, Marketing, etc., allowing users to explore relevant apps.

Using the search feature: Users can directly search for specific keywords or business problems to find matching apps.

Reading reviews and ratings: User feedback provides valuable insights into the effectiveness and reliability of different apps.

By combining these methods, users can efficiently identify and select the best-suited app for their business requirements.

Additional Considerations:

AppExchange also offers filters based on industry, company size, and other criteria to refine search results.

It's essential to evaluate the app's features, pricing, and compatibility before making a decision.

128] Answer: A) AppExchange

Explanation:

AppExchange is Salesforce's online marketplace for third-party applications and integrations. It provides a platform for businesses to discover, evaluate, and implement apps that can enhance their Salesforce organization's capabilities.

Why Other Options Are Incorrect:

Data Loader is a tool for importing and exporting data, not for integrating third-party applications.

Workflow Rules are used to automate business processes within Salesforce, not to integrate external systems.

Custom Objects are used to create custom data structures within Salesforce, but they don't facilitate integration with external apps.

By leveraging AppExchange, organizations can quickly and easily extend the functionality of Salesforce to meet specific business requirements without extensive development efforts.

129] Answer: D) All of the above

Explanation:

Reduced development time: AppExchange solutions are pre-built, so they eliminate the need for extensive custom development, saving time and resources.

Access to a wider range of tools: AppExchange offers a vast ecosystem of apps, providing businesses with access to specialized tools and functionalities beyond standard Salesforce features.

Prebuilt functionalities: AppExchange solutions come with ready-to-use features, allowing for faster implementation and immediate business value.

By leveraging AppExchange, organizations can accelerate their digital transformation and gain a competitive edge.

130] Answer: D) All of the above

Explanation:

Reading customer reviews: User feedback provides valuable insights into the app's performance, functionality, and overall satisfaction.

Checking provider certifications: Certifications indicate the provider's expertise and adherence to quality standards.

Testing in a sandbox environment: A sandbox allows users to evaluate the app's functionality and impact without affecting production data.

By thoroughly assessing these factors, users can make informed decisions about the suitability of an AppExchange solution for their organization.

131] Answer: A) Track service level agreements (SLAs)

Explanation:

Entitlements in Salesforce are used to define and track Service Level Agreements (SLAs) for customers. They represent the terms and conditions of a service contract, including details like support levels, response times, and escalation procedures.

Why Other Options Are Incorrect:

Manage customer accounts: This is primarily handled by the Accounts object in Salesforce.

Automate case routing: While entitlements can influence case routing based on SLA criteria, their primary purpose is to define SLAs.

Provide knowledge articles: Knowledge articles are managed separately within the Knowledge base.

Additional Considerations:

Entitlements can be linked to specific products, contracts, or customer tiers.

They can be used to prioritize cases based on SLA requirements.

Entitlements help ensure that customers receive the appropriate level of support.

By effectively using Entitlements, organizations can improve customer satisfaction and meet service level commitments.

132] Answer: C) Using Entitlements and Milestones

Explanation:

Entitlements define the service level agreements (SLAs) for customers, including response and resolution timeframes.

Milestones are used to track specific stages within a case's lifecycle, ensuring that cases progress through the resolution process within defined timeframes.

By setting milestones with associated due dates, you can monitor case progress and identify potential delays.

Why Other Options Are Incorrect:

Escalation Rules are used to automatically escalate cases based on certain criteria, but they don't directly enforce resolution timeframes.

Case Assignment Rules determine case ownership, but they don't impact case resolution timelines.

Workflow Rules can automate actions based on case criteria, but they are not specifically designed to track time-based targets.

By combining Entitlements and Milestones, organizations can effectively manage case SLAs and ensure timely resolution.

133] Answer: A) Knowledge Base

Explanation:

The Knowledge Base is a dedicated feature in Salesforce designed specifically for creating, managing, and sharing knowledge articles. It provides tools for authoring, publishing, and searching knowledge content to support both agents and customers.

Why Other Options Are Incorrect:

Content Library: While it might store documents, it's not primarily for creating and managing knowledge articles.

Document Manager: Similar to Content Library, it's for document storage and management, not knowledge articles.

Chatter Files: Used for sharing files within the organization, but not for structured knowledge management.

By utilizing the Knowledge Base, organizations can establish a centralized repository of information, improve customer self-service, and enhance agent productivity.

134] Answer: A) Define the terms of service for customers

Explanation:

A Service Contract in Salesforce outlines the specific terms and conditions of a service agreement between a company and its customers. It defines the services provided, the duration of the contract, pricing, and any associated SLAs or support levels.

Why Other Options Are Incorrect:

Manage customer accounts: While service contracts are related to customers, their primary purpose is to define the terms of service, not manage account information.

Track sales opportunities: Sales opportunities are handled through opportunities and quotes, not service contracts.

Schedule data backups: Data backups are typically managed through administrative settings and backup solutions, not service contracts.

Service Contracts are essential for managing customer expectations, enforcing service obligations, and providing a clear reference for both the company and the customer.

135] Answer: A) AutoResponse Rules

Explanation:

AutoResponse Rules are specifically designed to automate email responses based on incoming cases or emails. They allow you to create predefined email templates and set criteria for when those templates should be sent.

Why Other Options Are Incorrect:

Workflow Rules: While Workflow Rules can automate actions based on certain criteria, they are not specifically designed for sending automated email responses.

Approval Processes: Used for managing approval workflows, they do not handle automated email responses.

Process Builder: A more complex automation tool, Process Builder is not the ideal choice for simple, automated email responses.

By using AutoResponse Rules, businesses can improve response times, provide consistent information to customers, and free up agents to handle more complex inquiries.

136] Answer: A) Chatter

Explanation:

Chatter is Salesforce's social collaboration platform that enables users to communicate, share information, and collaborate on tasks and projects within the platform. It provides features like feeds, groups, files, and comments to facilitate teamwork and knowledge sharing.

Why Other Options Are Incorrect:

Activity Timeline: Primarily used to track interactions related to records, not for general collaboration.

Calendar: Primarily used for scheduling appointments, not for collaborative work.

Task Manager: While it manages tasks, it doesn't offer the same level of collaboration and communication features as Chatter.

Chatter is a central hub for team interaction, allowing for real-time updates, file sharing, and discussions around tasks and projects.

137] Answer: A) Provide a real-time collaboration space

Explanation:

The Chatter Feed is the heart of Salesforce's social collaboration platform. It offers a real-time stream of updates, posts, comments, and file sharing among users, groups, and records. This dynamic space fosters communication, knowledge sharing, and teamwork within an organization.

Why Other Options Are Incorrect:

Track sales performance: While Chatter can be used to share sales updates, it's not its primary function. Salesforce has dedicated tools for sales performance tracking.

Schedule tasks and events: Chatter is not a calendar or task management tool.

Manage user permissions: User permissions are managed through Salesforce's security settings, not Chatter.

Chatter's real-time nature and ability to connect people, information, and records make it a valuable tool for enhancing collaboration and productivity.

138] Answer: D) All of the above

Explanation:

Setting up email notifications: Users can configure email alerts for specific Chatter activities, ensuring they stay informed even when not actively using Salesforce.

Following relevant records and groups: By following records and groups, users receive updates whenever changes or new posts are made, keeping them engaged with the latest information.

Customizing their feed preferences: Users can tailor their Chatter feed to prioritize specific content, filtering out irrelevant updates and focusing on what matters most.

By combining these methods, users can effectively manage their Chatter feed and stay informed about critical updates and information.

139] Answer: A) Task Manager

Explanation:

The Task Manager is the dedicated feature in Salesforce for creating, assigning, prioritizing, and tracking tasks. It provides a centralized location to manage individual and team to-do lists.

Why Other Options Are Incorrect:

Activity Timeline is for tracking interactions related to records, not for managing tasks.

Calendar is for scheduling appointments and events, not for task management.

Chatter is a social collaboration tool, not primarily for task management.

The Task Manager is essential for staying organized and ensuring that tasks are completed on time.

140] Answer: A) Provide a historical view of activities related to a record

Explanation:

The Activity Timeline in Salesforce is a centralized location where you can view a chronological history of all interactions and activities associated with a specific record. This includes tasks, events, calls, emails, and other relevant information.

Why other options are incorrect:

B) Schedule future tasks and events: While you can view scheduled tasks and events in the Activity Timeline, its primary purpose is to provide a historical record, not for scheduling new ones.

C) Track sales opportunities: The Activity Timeline can be used to track activities related to sales opportunities, but it's not specifically designed for this purpose alone. It provides a broader view of all activities associated with a record.

D) Manage user permissions: User permissions are managed through Profiles and Permission Sets, not the Activity Timeline.

Additional Considerations:

The Activity Timeline replaced the Open Activities and Activity History related lists in Salesforce Classic.

It provides a visual and easy-to-understand view of all interactions with a record.

You can customize the Activity Timeline to display specific types of activities.

Einstein Activity Capture can automatically log activities to the Timeline.

By understanding the Activity Timeline, Salesforce users can gain valuable insights into the history of a record, improve collaboration, and make more informed decisions.

141] Answer: D) All of the above

Explanation:

Data Loader is a powerful tool in Salesforce designed to handle bulk data operations efficiently. It offers a versatile solution for managing large datasets.

Import large volumes of data: Data Loader can import massive amounts of data into Salesforce from various sources like CSV files or databases. This is particularly useful for initial data migration or regular data updates.

Export data to external systems: You can extract data from Salesforce and export it to external systems in a CSV format. This is beneficial for creating reports, analysis, or integration with other applications.

Perform bulk data updates: Data Loader allows you to update existing records in bulk, saving time and effort compared to manual updates. This is ideal for correcting data errors or making mass changes to records.

Additional Considerations:

Data Loader is a desktop application that needs to be installed on your computer.

It offers both a user interface and command-line interface for different user preferences.

There are limitations on the number of records and file size that can be processed using Data Loader.

For extremely large data volumes, consider using Salesforce Bulk API or other specialized tools.

By understanding the capabilities of Data Loader, Salesforce administrators can effectively manage data within the platform and streamline data integration processes.

142] Answer: B) Using Duplicate Rules

Explanation:

Duplicate Rules are specifically designed to identify and prevent duplicate records in Salesforce. They define matching criteria based on specific fields (like email, phone number, account name, etc.) and determine the action to be taken when a potential duplicate is found.

Why other options are incorrect:

A) Using Validation Rules: Validation Rules are used to enforce data integrity by checking data before saving a record. While they can help prevent invalid data, they are not specifically designed for duplicate prevention.

C) Using Workflow Rules: Workflow Rules are used to automate processes based on specific record changes. They are not intended for duplicate record detection.

D) Using Escalation Rules: Escalation Rules are used to assign tasks or send email alerts based on specific criteria. They do not address duplicate record issues.

Additional Considerations:

Duplicate Rules can be set up to block, alert, or allow duplicates with merging options.

You can define multiple Duplicate Rules for a single object.

Effective Duplicate Rules are essential for maintaining data quality and accuracy in Salesforce.

Consider using additional tools or techniques like data cleansing and deduplication processes for comprehensive duplicate management.

By implementing robust Duplicate Rules, organizations can significantly reduce the occurrence of duplicate records, improving data quality and overall Salesforce performance.

143] Answer: A) A rule to identify duplicate records

Explanation:

A Matching Rule in Salesforce defines the criteria used to identify potential duplicate records. It establishes the logic for comparing fields across records and determining if they are similar enough to be considered duplicates.

Why other options are incorrect:

B) A rule to merge duplicate records: Duplicate Rules, not Matching Rules, handle the merging of duplicate records after they've been identified.

C) A rule to update records: Workflow Rules or Process Builder are used for updating records based on specific conditions.

D) A rule to import records: Data Loader or Import Wizards are used for importing records into Salesforce.

Additional Considerations:

Matching Rules are the foundation for Duplicate Rules.

You can create custom Matching Rules for specific objects.

Salesforce provides standard Matching Rules for accounts, contacts, and leads.

Effective Matching Rules are crucial for maintaining data quality and preventing redundant records.

By understanding Matching Rules, Salesforce administrators can implement robust duplicate prevention strategies and improve overall data accuracy.

144] Answer: B) Duplicate Management

Explanation:

Duplicate Management is the comprehensive feature in Salesforce responsible for identifying, preventing, and merging duplicate records. It encompasses:

Matching Rules: Define the criteria for identifying potential duplicates.

Duplicate Rules: Specify actions to be taken when a potential duplicate is found (block, alert, or allow with merge options).

Duplicate Jobs: Run searches for existing duplicate records based on Matching Rules.

Duplicate Record Sets: Group identified duplicates for review and merging.

Why other options are incorrect:

A) Data Cleansing: While related to data quality, data cleansing focuses on correcting inaccurate or incomplete data, not specifically duplicates.

C) Data Quality Rules: These rules are for ensuring data accuracy and consistency, not specifically for duplicate management.

D) Data Merging: This is a specific action within Duplicate Management, not a feature itself.

By using Duplicate Management effectively, organizations can maintain data integrity, improve data accuracy, and enhance overall Salesforce performance.

145] Answer: D) Using Workflow Rules

Explanation:

While not the most efficient method for large-scale deletions, Workflow Rules can be used to automate the deletion of obsolete data in Salesforce under specific conditions. You can set up a Workflow Rule to delete records that meet certain criteria, such as a specific date field being older than a defined period.

Why other options are incorrect:

A) Using Data Export Service: This service is used to export data, not delete it.

B) Using Data Loader: Data Loader is a bulk import/export tool, not designed for automated deletion.

C) Using Mass Delete Records: This is a manual process, not automated.

Additional Considerations:

For large-scale deletions, Apex triggers or batch jobs are more efficient.

Careful consideration should be given to data retention policies and compliance requirements.

Testing is crucial to ensure the Workflow Rule functions as expected and doesn't delete important data.

Consider using scheduled jobs or Apex to automate the deletion process more effectively.

By carefully configuring Workflow Rules, you can automate the deletion of obsolete data to a certain extent, helping to maintain data cleanliness and storage efficiency. However, for more complex or high-volume deletion scenarios, exploring Apex-based solutions is recommended.

146] Answer: A) Highlight cells based on criteria

Explanation:

Conditional Highlighting is a feature in Salesforce reports that allows you to visually emphasize specific data points by applying colors to cells based on predefined criteria. This helps users quickly identify trends, outliers, or critical information within the report.

Why other options are incorrect:

B) Schedule report refreshes: Report subscriptions are used for scheduling report refreshes.

C) Customize report filters: Filters are used to refine the data displayed in a report.

D) Share reports with other users: Sharing options allow you to control who can access a report.

By using Conditional Highlighting, you can create more informative and visually appealing reports, making it easier for users to understand and analyze the data.

147] Answer: A) Summary Report

Explanation:

A Summary Report in Salesforce is the most suitable option for visualizing trends over time. It allows you to group data by time periods (e.g., days, weeks, months, quarters) and summarize the results using various functions like sum, average, count, etc. This enables you to create charts and graphs that effectively illustrate trends and patterns in your data.

Why other options are incorrect:

B) Tabular Report: A tabular report presents data in a spreadsheet-like format and is not ideal for visualizing trends over time.

C) Matrix Report: A matrix report is used for comparing data across multiple categories, not for visualizing trends over time.

D) Analytical Snapshot: An analytical snapshot is a static image of a report at a specific point in time, not suitable for showing trends.

Additional Considerations:

Summary reports can be further enhanced using chart formats like bar charts, line charts, and pie charts to provide a clear visual representation of trends.

You can customize the time period for grouping data to analyze trends at different intervals.

Summary reports are versatile and can be used for various data analysis purposes beyond trend analysis.

By effectively utilizing Summary Reports, Salesforce users can gain valuable insights into the performance of their business over time.

148] Answer: A) Categorize report records without creating a formula or custom field

Explanation:

A Bucket Field in Salesforce reports is a powerful tool that allows you to categorize data within a report without the need to create a custom formula field or modify the underlying object. It provides a flexible way to group report records based on specific criteria.

For example:

You can create a bucket field on the "Amount" field in an Opportunity report and categorize opportunities into buckets like "Low," "Medium," and "High" based on specific amount ranges.

You can create a bucket field on the "Close Date" field and categorize opportunities based on stages like "Pipeline," "Closing," and "Closed Won."

179

Why other options are incorrect:

B) Aggregate data from multiple fields: This is typically done using summary formulas or roll-up summaries.

C) Create cross object summaries: Cross-object summaries involve relationships between objects and are not related to bucket fields.

D) Set up report filters: Filters are used to narrow down the data displayed in a report, not categorize it.

By using Bucket Fields, you can create more insightful and actionable reports without altering your Salesforce data structure.

149] Answer: A) Using Field-Level Security

Explanation:

Field-Level Security is the most effective way to protect sensitive data from being exposed in reports. By controlling access to specific fields at the user or role level, you can prevent sensitive information from being displayed even if a user has access to the report itself.

Why other options are incorrect:

B) By creating private reports: While creating private reports limits access to the report itself, it doesn't prevent sensitive data from being included if the user has access to the underlying fields.

C) By applying report filters: Report filters can help exclude specific data from a report, but it might not be sufficient to protect sensitive information, especially if the filter criteria can be easily bypassed.

D) By using report folders: Report folders help organize reports but do not control data visibility.

Additional Considerations:

Combine Field-Level Security with other security features like role hierarchies, sharing settings, and data masking for comprehensive data protection.

Regularly review and update Field-Level Security settings to align with changing business requirements and security standards.

Consider using data classification and masking techniques for additional layers of protection.

By implementing robust Field-Level Security, organizations can safeguard sensitive data and comply with data privacy regulations.

150] Answer: B) Dynamic Dashboards

Explanation:

Dynamic Dashboards are the core tool for combining multiple reports into a single, interactive view in Salesforce. They provide a flexible and customizable way to present data from various sources in a visually appealing format.

Why other options are incorrect:

A) Report Snapshots: These are static images of reports at a specific point in time and cannot be combined on a single page.

C) Report Charts: These are visual representations of report data but cannot be combined independently on a single page.

D) Dashboard Components: While dashboards are made up of components, the term "dashboard components" doesn't accurately reflect the ability to combine multiple reports.

Additional Considerations:

Dashboards can include various components like charts, tables, metrics, and visual force pages to create comprehensive overviews.

Users can filter and drill down into data within a dashboard for further analysis.

Dashboards can be shared with other users or made public for broader access.

By leveraging Dynamic Dashboards, Salesforce users can create informative and engaging dashboards that provide valuable insights into their business.

151] Answer: C) Manage Users

Explanation:

The Manage Users permission grants a user the authority to create, edit, and manage other users within the Salesforce organization. This permission is typically assigned to system administrators or users with administrative responsibilities.

Why other options are incorrect:

A) View All Users: This permission only allows a user to view all users in the organization, but not create or modify them.

B) Modify All Data: While this permission grants extensive data modification rights, it does not specifically encompass user management.

D) Customize Application: This permission is related to customizing the Salesforce interface, not user management.

Additional Considerations:

The Manage Users permission is often combined with other administrative permissions for comprehensive control over the Salesforce environment.

Be cautious when granting this permission as it provides significant access to sensitive organizational data.

Consider using permission sets to grant specific user management capabilities without assigning the full Manage Users permission.

By understanding the Manage Users permission, administrators can effectively delegate user management responsibilities and maintain control over the Salesforce organization.

152] Answer: B) To import and export data

Explanation:

Data Loader is a powerful tool in Salesforce primarily used for efficiently handling large volumes of data. Its core functions include:

Importing data: Loading data into Salesforce from external sources like CSV files or databases.

Exporting data: Extracting data from Salesforce to external systems or creating data backups.

Why other options are incorrect:

A) To create custom objects: Custom objects are created using the Salesforce platform builder or metadata API.

C) To create validation rules: Validation rules are created through the Salesforce user interface or using the API.

D) To manage user profiles: User profiles are managed within the Salesforce user interface under the "Users" section.

Data Loader is essential for data migration, data synchronization, and bulk data operations in Salesforce.

153] Answer: B) Custom Fields

Explanation:

Custom fields are additional fields that you can add to standard objects (like Account, Contact, Opportunity) to store specific information that isn't captured by the standard fields. This allows you to tailor Salesforce to your organization's unique needs.

Why other options are incorrect:

A) Custom Objects: These are entirely new objects created for storing custom data, independent of standard objects.

C) Page Layouts: Page layouts control the visibility and placement of fields on record pages but don't create new fields.

D) Record Types: Record types define different sets of fields and business processes for a standard object but don't create new fields.

By creating custom fields, you can expand the functionality of standard objects and gather the specific data required for your business processes.

154] Answer: D) All of the above

Explanation:

Workflow rules are a powerful automation tool in Salesforce that can trigger various actions based on specific criteria. These actions include:

Sending an email alert: Notify users or stakeholders about specific record changes or events.

Creating a new record: Generate new records based on certain conditions (e.g., creating a task when an opportunity is closed won).

Updating a field value: Modify field values automatically based on specific criteria (e.g., changing a status field based on date).

By combining these actions, you can create complex automated processes to streamline your business operations.

155] Answer: C) Tabular Report

Explanation:

A Tabular Report in Salesforce presents data in a standard spreadsheet-like format with rows and columns. This type of report is ideal for displaying detailed information and is easy to read and understand.

Why other options are incorrect:

A) Summary Report: Provides a summary of data, often grouped by categories or time periods.

B) Matrix Report: Displays data in a matrix format, comparing data across multiple categories.

D) Joined Report: Combines data from multiple objects but doesn't necessarily display it in a tabular format.

Tabular reports are a fundamental report type in Salesforce for displaying raw data in a clear and organized manner.

156] Answer: B) To collaborate with colleagues

Explanation:

Chatter is Salesforce's social collaboration platform that allows users to connect and share information within the organization. It enables real-time communication, file sharing, and collaboration on various Salesforce records like opportunities, cases, and projects.

Why other options are incorrect:

A) To create custom reports: Reports are created using the reporting feature in Salesforce.

C) To manage user profiles: User profiles are managed in the user management section of Salesforce.

D) To import data: Data import is done using tools like Data Loader or the import wizard.

Chatter serves as a central hub for communication and knowledge sharing within a Salesforce organization.

157] Answer: B) Lightning Experience

Explanation:

Lightning Experience is Salesforce's modern, user-friendly interface designed to enhance productivity and user experience. It offers a responsive layout that adapts to different screen sizes, making it suitable for desktop, tablet, and mobile devices.

Why other options are incorrect:

A) Classic Experience: This is the older Salesforce interface, known for its less intuitive design and limited features.

C) Visual force Pages: While Visual force is used for custom page development, it's not the primary interface for end-users.

D) Apex Triggers: These are code-based triggers for automating actions and do not relate to the user interface.

Lightning Experience is Salesforce's recommended user interface for most organizations due to its improved usability, performance, and mobile optimization.

158] Answer: A) A marketplace for third-party apps

Explanation:

The AppExchange is Salesforce's online marketplace where you can find and install a wide range of applications, components, and services that extend the functionality of your Salesforce platform. It's like an app store for Salesforce, offering solutions for various business needs.

Why other options are incorrect:

B) A feature to create custom objects: Custom objects are created within your Salesforce org using the platform builder.

C) A tool for data migration: Data Loader is a tool specifically designed for data migration.

D) A module for user training: Salesforce offers training resources and certifications, but not through the AppExchange.

By leveraging the AppExchange, businesses can quickly adopt solutions to address specific challenges without the need to build everything from scratch.

159] Answer: B) To track sales leads and opportunities

Explanation:

Sales Cloud is the core component of Salesforce designed specifically to manage and optimize the sales process. Its primary function is to track and nurture leads, manage sales opportunities, and ultimately close deals.

Why other options are incorrect:

A) To manage customer service cases: This is primarily the function of Service Cloud.

C) To create custom reports: While Sales Cloud can generate reports, its core focus is on sales management.

D) To manage user profiles: User profiles are managed within the Salesforce admin settings.

Sales Cloud provides a comprehensive platform for sales teams to increase productivity, improve forecasting, and drive revenue growth.

160] Answer: A) Knowledge Base

Explanation:

A Knowledge Base is a centralized repository of information that empowers agents to quickly find solutions to customer inquiries. It contains articles, FAQs, and other relevant content that can be easily searched and accessed, reducing the need for agents to repeatedly research the same information.

Why other options are incorrect:

B) Chatter: While Chatter is useful for collaboration, it's not primarily designed for quickly finding solutions to customer issues.

C) Reports and Dashboards: These are tools for analyzing data and performance, not for direct customer interaction.

D) Workflow Rules: Workflow rules automate tasks based on specific criteria but are not directly involved in handling customer inquiries.

A robust Knowledge Base is essential for improving customer satisfaction, increasing agent productivity, and reducing case resolution times.

161] Answer: B) To collaborate with external users

Explanation:

A Salesforce Community is designed to facilitate interaction and collaboration between your organization and external stakeholders such as customers, partners, or employees. It provides a platform for sharing information, knowledge, and resources, fostering a sense of community and improving overall engagement.

Why other options are incorrect:

A) To manage user profiles: User profiles are managed within the Salesforce admin settings.

C) To create custom objects: Custom objects are created using the Salesforce platform builder.

D) To import data: Data import is done using tools like Data Loader or the import wizard.

By creating a community, businesses can enhance customer satisfaction, strengthen partner relationships, and streamline communication.

162] Answer: C) Record Type

Explanation:

Record Types are used to define different sets of fields, page layouts, validation rules, and other settings for a standard or custom object. By utilizing Record Types, an administrator can specify different picklist values based on the specific type of opportunity. This ensures that users see only relevant options when creating or editing an opportunity.

Breakdown of other options:

A) Fields and Relationships: This is used to define the structure of the object and its relationships with other objects. It does not control picklist values based on record type.

B) Related lookup filters: These are used to control which records are displayed in a lookup field based on specific criteria. This is not related to picklist values.

D) Picklist value sets: While picklist value sets can be used to manage picklist values, they do not provide a mechanism to control which values are available based on record type.

By using Record Types, Cloud Kicks can effectively manage different picklist options for various opportunity types, improving data accuracy and user experience.

163] D) Flow Builder

Explanation:

Flow Builder is the ideal tool for creating a multi-step form or wizard to capture information about a lost client. It offers flexibility in designing user interfaces, collecting data, and performing actions based on user input.

You can create screens with various input fields, decision points, and even incorporate logic to guide users through the process.

Flow Builder also allows for integration with other Salesforce components and external systems, making it a versatile solution for complex business processes.

Breakdown of other options:

Process Builder is primarily used for automating processes based on record changes, not for creating interactive forms.

Approval Process is specifically for routing records through an approval workflow, not for data collection.

Outbound Message is used to send data to external systems, not to capture data from users.

By using Flow Builder, the administrator can create a user-friendly form that efficiently collects the required information about the lost client.

164] Answer: B) Validation Rule

Explanation:

A Validation Rule is the correct choice to prevent sales team members from setting an opportunity close date to a past date.

Validation Rules enforce data integrity by preventing invalid data from being saved. In this case, we can create a validation rule that checks if the Close Date is less than or equal to today's date. If it is, an error message will be displayed, preventing the user from saving the record.

Breakdown of other options:

Assignment Rule is used to automatically assign records to users or queues based on specific criteria.

Field-Level Security controls access to specific fields, but it doesn't prevent users from entering invalid data.

Approval Process is used to route records through an approval workflow, not to enforce data validation.

By implementing a validation rule, the administrator can ensure that opportunity close dates are always accurate and future-oriented.

165] Northern Trail Outfitters wants to track ROI for key stakeholder contacts on opportunities and make this data accessible for reporting directly from the opportunity.

Correct Answers:

D) Customize Opportunity Contact Role.

E) Add the Opportunity Contact Role related list to the Opportunity page layout.

Explanation:

Opportunity Contact Role:

This object specifically defines the role of a contact in relation to an opportunity.

It allows you to assign different roles to contacts (e.g., Decision Maker, Influencer, Economic Buyer).

You can track information related to each contact's role, such as their influence on the deal, their involvement in the sales process, and their expected ROI.

Adding the Opportunity Contact Role related list to the Opportunity page layout:

This makes the information about contacts and their roles directly accessible from the opportunity record.

The sales team can easily view and update contact roles and related information without navigating to separate records.

This data can then be used for reporting and analysis.

Why other options are incorrect:

A) Customize Campaign Member Role: This is irrelevant as the requirement is to track ROI for contacts on opportunities, not campaigns.

B) Add the Campaign Member related list to the Opportunity page layout: Similar to option A, this option is not related to tracking contacts on opportunities.

C) Customize Campaign Role: Again, this option is related to campaigns and not opportunities.

Additional Considerations:

Custom Fields: You might need to create custom fields on the Opportunity Contact Role object to capture specific ROI-related data, such as expected revenue, cost, and ROI calculation.

Reporting: Create custom reports and dashboards to analyze the ROI data based on contact roles and opportunity stages.

Workflow Rules and Approvals: You can set up workflow rules or approval processes based on contact roles and ROI metrics.

Data Validation: Implement data validation rules to ensure data accuracy and consistency.

By following these steps, Northern Trail Outfitters can effectively track and analyze ROI for key stakeholder contacts on opportunities, providing valuable insights for sales management.

166] Universal Containers has a single support process with 10 status values for all case types. This is causing confusion and inefficiency for service reps who only need up to five statuses per case type.

Correct Answer:

C) Review which status choices are needed for each record type and create support processes for each that is necessary.

Explanation:

By creating separate support processes for different case types, the administrator can tailor the status values to the specific needs of each process. This will significantly improve the user experience by reducing the number of irrelevant status options for service reps.

Why other options are incorrect:

A) Reduce the number of case status values to five: This is a blanket approach that might not be suitable for all case types. Some case types might require more than five statuses.

B) Create a Screen Flow: While Screen Flows can be used to customize user interfaces, they are not the best fit for this scenario. Creating multiple support processes is a more structural and efficient solution.

D) Edit the status choices directly on the record type: This is not possible in Salesforce. Status values are defined within a support process, not at the record type level.

Additional Considerations:

Case Record Types: Ensure that the case record types accurately reflect the different types of cases being handled.

Status Value Mapping: If there are overlapping status values between different support processes, consider creating a mapping table to standardize reporting.

User Training: Provide adequate training to service reps on the new support processes and status values.

Testing: Thoroughly test the new support processes to ensure they function as expected.

By following these guidelines, Universal Containers can streamline its case management process and enhance user satisfaction.

167] Northern Trail Outfitters needs to:

Generate expense reports in Salesforce.

Route these reports for approval by both managers and directors.

Send approved reports to an external HR system.

Correct Answers:

C. Approval Process

B. Outbound Message

Explanation:

Approval Process:

This tool is specifically designed to route records through a defined workflow for approval.

It can be configured to send expense reports to managers and directors for review and approval.

Approval processes can include multiple levels of approval, which is necessary for both managers and directors to review the expense report.

Outbound Message:

Once the expense report has been approved, an outbound message can be used to send the data to the external HR system.

Outbound messages can be triggered based on specific criteria, such as the approval status of the expense report.

Why other options are incorrect:

A. Quick Action: While quick actions can streamline record creation, they are not suitable for complex approval processes or data integration with external systems.

D. Email Alert Action: Email alerts are primarily for notifications and do not handle complex workflows or data transfer.

Additional Considerations:

Data Mapping: Ensure that the data fields in Salesforce align with the expected format in the HR system.

Error Handling: Implement error handling mechanisms to address potential issues during the outbound message process.

Testing: Thoroughly test the approval process and outbound message to identify and resolve any issues.

By using Approval Processes and Outbound Messages, Northern Trail Outfitters can effectively manage expense report approvals and integration with the HR system.

168] Correct Answer: A. Geolocation

Explanation:

Geolocation is the most suitable field type for recording geographic coordinates (latitude and longitude). This field specifically stores location data, making it ideal for tracking the movement of shipments.

Salesforce provides built-in functionalities to visualize geolocation data on maps, allowing for easy tracking and analysis.

Why other options are incorrect:

B. Geofence: A geofence defines a virtual geographic boundary, which is not suitable for tracking the movement of shipments.

C. Custom Address: While a custom address field can store address information, it doesn't directly capture geographic coordinates, which are essential for precise location tracking.

D. External Lookup: This field type is used to reference data from an external system, not for storing geographic information.

By using a Geolocation field, Cloud Kicks can effectively track the location of its shipments, providing valuable insights into delivery times, routes, and potential issues.

169] Correct Answers:

B. Standard objects are provided by default with Salesforce.

A. Custom and standard objects come with predefined fields.

Explanation:

Standard objects: These are pre-built objects that come with Salesforce out-of-the-box, such as Accounts, Contacts, Leads, Opportunities, etc. They are foundational to most Salesforce implementations.

Custom and standard objects: Both types of objects have predefined fields. Standard objects come with default fields, while custom objects allow you to define your own fields.

Why other options are incorrect:

C. It is possible to create a new standard object: This is incorrect. You cannot create new standard objects.

D. Master-detail relationships are supported only by standard objects: This is also incorrect. Both standard and custom objects can have master-detail relationships.

Understanding these factors is essential for designing and implementing effective data structures within Salesforce.

170] Correct Answers:

A. The report requires refreshing.

D. There are different permissions for the running dashboard user and the viewer.

Explanation:

The report requires refreshing: If the underlying data for the report has changed since the dashboard was last refreshed, the figures on the report and dashboard will differ. A manual refresh of the report will synchronize the data.

Different permissions: Users might have different access levels to the data used in the report. This can result in different data subsets being displayed for different users, leading to discrepancies between the dashboard and the report.

Why other options are incorrect:

B. The dashboard requires refreshing: Refreshing the dashboard would not resolve the issue if the underlying report data is outdated.

C. The current user lacks access to the report folder: This would prevent the user from accessing the detailed report altogether, not just showing incorrect figures.

By addressing these two potential causes, the administrator can help ensure data consistency between dashboards and reports.

171] Correct Answers:

B. Edit the picklist values for Campaign Status in Object Manager.

C. Use mass modification for the Campaign Member Statuses related list.

Explanation:

To add a new picklist value to the Campaign Member Status field, you need to modify the field itself, not the related list.

Edit the picklist values for Campaign Status in Object Manager: This is where you can add, edit, or remove values from the Campaign Member Status picklist.

Use mass modification for the Campaign Member Statuses related list: Once you've added the new value, you can use mass modification to update existing records with the new status if needed.

Why other options are incorrect:

A. Add the Campaign Member Statuses related list to the Page Layout: This will only display the related list on the page layout, but it doesn't allow you to modify the picklist values.

D. Change the picklist value directly on the Campaign Member Statuses related list: You cannot modify picklist values directly on a related list.

By following these steps, the administrator can effectively add a new picklist value to the Campaign Member Status field and update existing records if necessary.

172] Correct Answers:

B. Case

E. Account

Explanation:

Case: This is the core object for managing customer support issues. It tracks details like the customer, issue description, status, and resolution.

Account: This object represents the customer or organization that is receiving support. It stores information like company name, address, contact details, etc.

Why other options are incorrect:

A. Contract: This object is typically used for managing contractual agreements and is not directly related to support cases.

C. Ticket: Salesforce doesn't have a standard "Ticket" object. It's common to use Cases for this purpose.

D. Request: This is a generic term and not a specific standard object in Salesforce.

By utilizing the Case and Account objects, Ursa Solar Major can effectively manage its customer support operations within Salesforce.

173] Correct Answer: B. Set up three auto-response rules, configuring one rule entry criterion for each rule and applying a filter based on case priority. Select the corresponding email template for each rule entry.

Explanation:

Auto-response rules are specifically designed to send automated email responses based on specific criteria.

Creating three separate auto-response rules allows for distinct configurations for each case priority level (low, medium, high).

Each rule can have a single rule entry criterion based on case priority, ensuring accurate email template selection.

Why other options are incorrect:

A. Assignment rules: These are used to assign cases to users or queues, not for sending automated emails.

C. Workflow rule: While workflow rules can send email alerts, they are more complex and not ideal for simple automated email responses based on specific criteria.

D. Single auto-response rule with three rule entry criteria: This approach could be used, but it's less efficient and potentially more error-prone compared to creating three separate rules.

By using three auto-response rules, Ursa Major Solar can effectively send tailored email notifications to customers based on case priority, improving customer satisfaction and communication.

174] Correct Answer: D. Gauge

Explanation:

A gauge is the ideal component to visually represent a single value and its progress towards a goal.

It can clearly display the total sales for the year as the current value and the enterprise sales goal as the maximum value.

The gauge's needle or indicator will show the percentage of the goal achieved, providing a quick and easy-to-understand visual representation.

Why other options are incorrect:

Table: While a table can display the information, it's not visually impactful and doesn't provide a clear overview of progress towards the goal.

Stacked Bar: A stacked bar chart is better suited for comparing multiple categories within a single value, not for showing progress towards a single goal.

Donut: A donut chart is effective for showing proportions of different categories within a whole, but it's not the best choice for displaying a single value and its progress towards a goal.

A gauge effectively communicates the key metric (total sales) and its relationship to the target (enterprise sales goal) in a single, easy-to-understand visual.

175] Correct Answer: D. Distinct record types and sales processes for each type of opportunity.

Explanation:

Creating separate record types and sales processes for business and partner opportunities is the most effective way to manage distinct sales processes with different stages, page layouts, and picklist values.

Distinct record types: This allows for different page layouts, fields, and picklist values for each type of opportunity.

Separate sales processes: This enables you to define unique stages, probability calculations, and other process-specific settings for each opportunity type.

Why other options are incorrect:

A. Validation rules: While validation rules can ensure data accuracy, they don't address the fundamental differences between the two opportunity types.

B. Separate page layouts: Page layouts can customize the user interface but don't handle the underlying process differences.

C. Public groups: Public groups are used for sharing records and don't provide the necessary structure for different opportunity types.

By using distinct record types and sales processes, Northern Trail Outfitters can effectively manage the unique requirements of their business and partner opportunities.

176] Correct Answer: A. Use a muting permission set to disable specific permissions within the permission set group.

Explanation:

A muting permission set is designed specifically to override permissions from other permission sets or permission set groups. In this case, we want to override the Delete permissions granted by the managed package's permission set group.

By creating a muting permission set and removing the Delete permissions for the specific objects, the administrator can effectively prevent users in the permission set group from deleting records without affecting other permissions granted by the managed package.

Why other options are incorrect:

B. Create a new permission set without Delete access: This would require assigning a new permission set to users, which can be time-consuming and might impact other permissions.

C. Establish a new role: Roles are hierarchical and determine object-level permissions. They are not ideal for granular control over specific permissions like Delete.

D. Modify the users' profiles: Modifying user profiles can have unintended consequences on other permissions and is not recommended, especially when dealing with managed packages.

Using a muting permission set provides the most granular control and minimizes potential side effects.

177] Correct Answer: B. Configure a validation rule that requires Lead Source to be selected when the stage is set to "Closed Won."

Explanation:

A validation rule is the most appropriate tool for enforcing this business requirement. It allows you to define specific conditions under which a record can be saved. In this case, the condition would be:

If the Opportunity Stage is "Closed Won", then Lead Source must not be blank.

If the condition is not met, an error message will be displayed, preventing the user from saving the record until the Lead Source is filled in.

Why other options are incorrect:

A. Set up Lead Source as a dependent picklist for the Opportunity stage field: Dependent pick lists limit the available values in one field based on the selection in another. This doesn't enforce a mandatory requirement for Lead Source when the stage is "Closed Won."

C. Change the Opportunity stage field to read-only on the page layout: Making the stage field read-only would prevent users from changing the stage, which is not the desired outcome.

D. Modify the Opportunity stage field to be a dependent picklist based on the Lead Source field: This would restrict the available stage options based on the Lead Source, which is not the requirement.

By implementing a validation rule, Cloud Kicks can ensure data integrity and prevent invalid Opportunity records from being created.

178] Correct Answers:

A. Add a path for the Stage field to the Opportunity record page.

D. Create a simplified Opportunity page layout.

Explanation:

The primary issue is that users are experiencing delays when updating the Stage field on Opportunity records. To address this, the administrator should focus on streamlining the Opportunity record page and making the Stage field more accessible.

Add a path for the Stage field to the Opportunity record page: This places the Stage field at the top of the page, making it easily accessible and reducing the need to scroll.

Create a simplified Opportunity page layout: By removing unnecessary fields from the page layout, the administrator can reduce page load times and improve overall performance. This is especially effective if users primarily interact with the Stage field.

Why other options are incorrect:

B. Utilize a Kanban list view for Opportunities: While Kanban views are helpful for visualizing the sales pipeline, they don't directly address the issue of slow Stage field updates.

C. Set up an auto-launched flow to simplify Opportunity editing: While flows can automate processes, they might introduce additional complexity and potentially slow down the user experience in this case.

By implementing these two changes, the administrator can significantly improve the performance and user experience when updating Opportunity Stages.

179] Correct Answer: C. Use the $Record global variable.

Explanation:

199

The $Record global variable is specifically designed to reference the record that triggered the flow. In this case, since the flow is triggered on a Contact record, the $Record variable will contain all the field values of the active Contact record.

Here's an example of how you can use the $Record variable to access a specific field:

Why other options are incorrect:

A. {!Contact.Id} global variable: This would only provide the Contact ID, not all the field values.

B. {!Account.Id} record variable: This assumes the flow is updating an Account record, which is not the case based on the question.

D. Use the Get Records element to find the Id: This would be unnecessarily complex. The $Record variable provides direct access to the triggered record's information.

180] A user needs to be immediately removed from Salesforce due to a request from HR. This user is also referenced as a 'Direct Manager' for other employees.

Correct Answer: A. Freeze the user to prevent them from logging in

Explanation:

Freezing a user is the most appropriate action in this scenario because it:

Immediately prevents the user from accessing Salesforce: This addresses the urgent requirement from HR.

Preserves the user's data and relationships: Freezing the user maintains their data, including the 'Direct Manager' references, allowing for future changes or reactivation if needed.

Why other options are incorrect:

B. Deactivate the user and delete any records where they are referenced in the Direct Manager field: Deactivating a user is not immediate and deleting records can lead to data loss and inconsistencies.

C. Change the user's profile to read-only while removing them from being referenced in the Direct Manager Field: Making a user read-only is not sufficient to prevent access and removing them from 'Direct Manager' might not be possible immediately due to dependencies.

D. Delete the user and leave all records where they referenced in the Direct Manager Field without changes: Deleting a user permanently removes their data and breaks relationships, which is not ideal in this situation.

Additional Considerations:

Communication with HR: Clarify the reason for the immediate access removal to determine if freezing is indeed the best course of action.

Documentation: Record the reason for freezing the user and any relevant details for future reference.

Follow-up: Establish a plan for either reactivating or fully deactivating the user after the situation is resolved.

By freezing the user, the administrator addresses the urgent request while minimizing potential negative impacts.

181]Answer: D. Enable Contacts to multiple Accounts.

Explanation:

AWC wants to maintain historical accuracy of the Contact record: This means they need to keep the original Contact record intact, even when the contractor changes agencies.

Contractors often change agencies: This indicates a many-to-many relationship between Contacts and Accounts (one Contact can belong to multiple Accounts, and one Account can have multiple Contacts).

By enabling Contacts to multiple Accounts, AWC can:

- Maintain a single Contact record for each contractor, preserving historical data.
- Associate the Contact with multiple Accounts (agencies) over time.
- Track the contractor's relationship with different agencies accurately.

This approach provides flexibility and data integrity for managing contractors who frequently change agencies.

Other options:

A. Use a partner community: Not applicable as it's for external users, not internal tracking.

B. Create a new Contact record for each agency: Inefficient and creates redundant data.

C. Create a Junction object: While this could work, it's overkill for this scenario as Salesforce already supports Contacts with multiple Accounts.

Therefore, D. Enable Contacts to multiple Accounts is the most suitable option.

182] Case escalation rules are automated processes that trigger actions when a case meets specific criteria (e.g., age, status, priority). They are primarily used to manage case SLAs, improve response times, and ensure cases are handled efficiently.

Correct Answers:

B. Send email notifications: This is a common action to alert relevant parties (case owners, supervisors, customers) about the case escalation.

D. Re-assign the Case: Escalation often involves transferring the case to a higher-level support team or individual for faster resolution.

Incorrect Answers:

A. Re-open the Case: Re-opening a case is typically done manually when a previously closed case is reopened by a customer. Escalation rules focus on moving a case forward, not reversing its status.

C. Change the Case Priority: While priority might be a factor in determining when a case escalates, changing the priority is not a typical action within an escalation rule. It's more likely that the escalation rule is triggered based on an existing priority level.

Example:

A customer support team uses case escalation rules to manage case SLAs. Cases with a priority of "High" that remain open for more than 24 hours will be escalated. The escalation rule triggers two actions:

Send an email notification to the case owner and their supervisor.

Re-assign the case to a Tier 2 support team.

Additional Considerations:

Escalation rules can be combined with other automation tools like workflow rules and approval processes for a comprehensive case management strategy.

Careful consideration should be given to escalation criteria, actions, and notification recipients to avoid overwhelming users with unnecessary alerts.

Regularly review and adjust escalation rules to ensure they align with changing business needs and SLAs.

By understanding these concepts, you can effectively use case escalation rules to improve case handling efficiency and customer satisfaction.

183] The sales director at Cloud Kicks needs tools to predict future revenue and measure sales rep performance.

Correct Answers:

C. Forecasting: This feature is specifically designed to predict future revenue by analyzing the pipeline of opportunities. It allows sales managers to set quotas, track progress, and identify potential issues.

D. Opportunity Stages: These define the different stages an opportunity goes through from initial contact to closed-won. Accurate opportunity stage management is crucial for forecasting as it provides insights into the likelihood of closing a deal.

Incorrect Answers:

A. Sales Quotes: While sales quotes are essential for the sales process, they are not directly used for revenue prediction. They represent potential deals but do not provide a probabilistic view of closing.

B. Opportunity List View: A list view is a way to filter and display opportunities. While useful for managing opportunities, it doesn't provide predictive capabilities or performance metrics.

Explanation:

By configuring forecasting and defining accurate opportunity stages, the sales director can:

- Predict future revenue: Forecasting provides a clear picture of expected revenue based on the opportunity pipeline and stage probabilities.
- Set goals: Based on the forecast, the sales director can set realistic revenue targets for the team and individual reps.
- Benchmark rep performance: Comparing actual sales to forecasted amounts allows for evaluating sales rep performance and identifying areas for improvement.

Additional Considerations:

- Forecast Categories: Consider creating forecast categories to group opportunities based on probability of closing.
- Forecast Types: Explore different forecast types (e.g., opportunity-based, collaborative) to find the best fit for your organization.
- Regular Review: Regularly review and adjust forecast settings to ensure accuracy and alignment with business goals.

By effectively utilizing forecasting and opportunity stages, Cloud Kicks can improve sales planning, performance management, and overall revenue predictability.

184] Universal Containers needs to display different Lightning pages for Accounts when viewed from the Sales Console and Service Console.

Correct Answer:

A. Update page layout assignments.

Explanation:

Page layout assignments determine which page layout is used for a specific record type.

By creating different page layouts for Accounts in the Sales and Service Consoles and assigning them to appropriate record types, the administrator can achieve the desired result.

Incorrect Answers:

B. Define multiple record types: While record types can be used to differentiate data based on specific criteria, they are not directly tied to console-specific page layouts.

C. Assign Lightning pages as app default: App default pages determine the initial page displayed when a record is created or edited, but they don't control which page is shown in different consoles.

D. Create different user profiles: User profiles control access to objects, fields, and other Salesforce features, but they don't determine the specific page layout displayed in a console.

Example:

Create two record types for Accounts: Sales Account and Service Account.

Create two different Lightning page layouts: Sales Account Layout and Service Account Layout.

Assign the Sales Account Layout to the Sales Account record type and the Service Account Layout to the Service Account record type.

Configure the Sales Console to use the Sales Account record type and the Service Console to use the Service Account record type.

By following these steps, the system will automatically display the correct Lightning page based on the console being used.

Additional Considerations:

Ensure that the page layouts include the necessary components and fields for each console's specific needs.

Consider using Lightning App Builder to create custom Lightning pages that meet the unique requirements of each console.

Test the configuration thoroughly to verify that the correct pages are displayed in both consoles.

By effectively utilizing page layout assignments, Universal Containers can provide a tailored user experience for their sales and service teams.

185] Sales reps at Northern Trail Outfitters want to be able to manually adjust the Probability field on Opportunity records.

Correct Answer:

D. Make the field editable on page layouts

Explanation:

By default, the Probability field is calculated based on the Opportunity Stage. To allow sales reps to manually override this value, the administrator needs to make the Probability field editable on the relevant opportunity page layouts.

Incorrect Answers:

A. Define a new Stage picklist value: Creating a new stage would not allow sales reps to manually change the probability.

B. Create a custom field on Opportunity: Creating a custom field would duplicate functionality and introduce unnecessary complexity.

C. Configure Forecasting support: Forecasting support is unrelated to the ability to edit the Probability field.

Additional Considerations:

Impact on Forecasting: Making the Probability field editable might affect forecasting accuracy if sales reps frequently override the system-generated values.

User Training: Provide clear guidelines to sales reps on when and why they should manually adjust the Probability field.

Field Validation: Consider adding field validation rules to ensure that Probability values are within a specific range (e.g., 0-100).

By making the Probability field editable, sales reps have more flexibility in managing their opportunities, while the administrator can monitor its impact on forecasting accuracy.

186] B. Get Records

Explanation:

Get Records is the specific flow element designed to retrieve records based on defined criteria.

It allows you to specify the object to query, filter the results based on conditions, and store the retrieved records in a collection variable.

You can then iterate through the collection and extract specific values into individual variables for subsequent use in the flow.

Why other options are incorrect:

Assignment: Used to assign values to variables but doesn't retrieve data from Salesforce.

Create Records: Used to create new records, not retrieve existing ones.

Update Records: Used to modify existing records, not retrieve data.

By using the Get Records element, the administrator can efficiently fetch the required data and proceed with the flow logic.

187] D. The flow trigger is missing.

Explanation:

A flow trigger is essential for initiating a flow. Without a trigger, the flow won't start, and consequently, no new records will be created.

Why other options are incorrect:

A. The flow is read only: A read-only flow would prevent updates or creations, but it would still be activated.

B. The flow is inactive: An inactive flow wouldn't run at all.

C. The flow URL is deactivated: Flow URLs are used for screen flows, not for record-triggered flows.

Therefore, the most likely cause for the issue is a missing flow trigger.

188] A master-detail relationship is a strong link between two objects. The master object is the parent, and the detail object is the child. Changes made to the master record automatically cascade to the detail records.

Correct Answers:

A. The master object can be a standard or custom object.

D. Roll-up summaries are supported in master-detail relationships.

E. The owner field on the detail records is the owner of the master record.

Explanation:

A. The master object can be a standard or custom object.

This is true. Both standard Salesforce objects (like Account, Contact, Opportunity) and custom objects can be the master in a master-detail relationship. For example, you could have a master-detail relationship between an Account (standard) and a Custom Object like 'Project'.

D. Roll-up summaries are supported in master-detail relationships.

Roll-up summaries allow you to calculate summary information from related records and display it on the master record. For instance, you can calculate the total amount of all Opportunities associated with an Account. This feature is exclusive to master-detail relationships.

E. The owner field on the detail records is the owner of the master record.

In a master-detail relationship, the ownership is inherited. The detail records automatically take on the owner of the master record. This ensures data integrity and security.

Why other options are incorrect:

B. Permissions for the detail record are set independently of the master.

This is false. Security permissions for detail records are inherited from the master record. If a user has access to the master record, they automatically have access to its related detail records.

C. Each object can have up to five master-detail relationships.

There's no limit to the number of master-detail relationships an object can have. You can create as many as needed to represent your business processes.

Additional Considerations:

Master-detail relationships enforce data integrity by preventing deletion of a master record if there are related detail records.

They are essential for creating hierarchical data structures, such as account hierarchies.

Understanding master-detail relationships is crucial for designing efficient Salesforce data models.

By understanding these characteristics, you can effectively model your business processes and create robust Salesforce applications.

189] The administrator aims to restrict Salesforce access to within the company's network. This is a security measure to protect sensitive data.

Correct Answers:

A. IP address restrictions are set on the profile or globally for the org.

C. Enforce Login IP Ranges on Every Request must be selected to enforce IP restrictions.

Explanation:

A. IP address restrictions are set on the profile or globally for the org.

This is a core configuration for limiting access based on IP addresses. You can define specific IP ranges allowed to access Salesforce. This can be set at a profile level for granular control or globally for the entire organization.

C. Enforce Login IP Ranges on Every Request must be selected to enforce IP restrictions.

This setting ensures that the IP restrictions defined are enforced for every login attempt. Without this, users might be able to bypass IP restrictions in certain scenarios.

Why other options are incorrect:

B. Users can change their password to avoid login IP restrictions.

Changing a password does not bypass IP restrictions. IP restrictions are based on the device's IP address, not user credentials.

D. Single sign-on will allow users to log in from anywhere.

Single sign-on simplifies the login process but doesn't inherently change the location from where the user is accessing Salesforce. IP restrictions still apply in this case.

Additional Considerations:

IP Range Management: Carefully define IP ranges to avoid blocking legitimate access. Consider using IP ranges instead of single IP addresses for flexibility.

- VPN Considerations: If users need to access Salesforce remotely, ensure that VPN connections are configured to use allowed IP ranges.
- Exception Handling: Create a process to handle exceptions, such as when users need to access Salesforce from outside the network for specific reasons.

By implementing IP restrictions and enforcing them consistently, the administrator can significantly enhance the security of Salesforce data.

190] An approval process is a workflow that guides a record through a series of steps before it's finalized. Automated actions are tasks that can be performed automatically at specific points in the approval process.

Correct Answers:

A. Field Update

D. Email Alert

Explanation:

A. Field Update: This action allows you to automatically change the value of a field on the record when specific conditions are met. For example, you could update the "Status" field to "Approved" or "Rejected" based on the approval outcome.

D. Email Alert: You can send email notifications to specific users or groups when certain events occur in the approval process. For example, you could send an email to the employee when their time off request is approved or rejected.

Why other options are incorrect:

B. Chatter Post: While Chatter is a powerful tool for collaboration, it's not an available automated action within an approval process.

C. Auto-launched Flow: Auto-launched flows can be triggered by approval processes, but they are not a direct automated action within the approval process itself.

Additional Considerations:

You can add multiple automated actions to an approval process step.

The order of automated actions matters.

Consider using conditional actions to execute automated actions based on specific criteria.

By effectively using field updates and email alerts, you can streamline the time-off approval process and improve communication.

191] Marking a field as required ensures that a value must be entered for that field before a record can be saved. This is essential for data integrity and to ensure critical information is captured.

Correct Answers:

B. The field is universally required to save a record on that object.

D. The field is optional when saving records via web-to-lead and web-to-case.

Explanation:

B. The field is universally required to save a record on that object.

This is the core implication of marking a field as required. It applies to all methods of saving records, including the user interface, API, and bulk data loads.

D. The field is optional when saving records via web-to-lead and web-to-case.

While a field is required for standard record creation, it's typically optional for web-to-lead and web-to-case processes. This is because these processes often involve capturing limited information from a web form.

Why other options are incorrect:

A. The field is not required to save records via the API on that object.

This is incorrect. As mentioned earlier, a required field is enforced across all methods of saving records, including the API.

C. The field is added to every page layout on that object.

While it's common practice to include required fields on page layouts, it's not a direct consequence of marking a field as required. You can choose which fields to display on each page layout independently.

Additional Considerations:

Be cautious when making fields universally required as it can impact data entry efficiency and user experience.

Consider using validation rules to enforce specific data requirements without making fields universally required.

For web-to-lead and web-to-case processes, carefully select which fields to make required to balance data capture and user experience.

By understanding these considerations, you can effectively use required fields to improve data quality and consistency in your Salesforce org.

192] Answer: C. Utility Bar

Explanation:

Utility Bar: This is a mobile-specific component designed to provide quick access to essential actions and information within the Salesforce Mobile App. It's specifically tailored for the smaller screen size and touch-based interactions of mobile devices.

Why other options are incorrect:

211

A. Today: This is a standard component accessible in both Lightning Experience and the Salesforce Mobile App.

B. Favorites: Similar to Today, Favorites is available in both Lightning Experience and the Salesforce Mobile App.

D. Home Page: The Home page is the starting point for a Salesforce user, but its layout and components can differ between Lightning Experience and the Salesforce Mobile App.

By understanding the specific components designed for mobile devices, you can create Lightning Apps that provide an optimal user experience for your mobile users.

193] Correct Answers:

A. Users need to connect an authenticator app to their Salesforce account.

D. Users need to enter a verification code from email or SMS, whichever has higher priority.

Explanation:

A. Users need to connect an authenticator app to their Salesforce account.

This is a common method for two-factor authentication (2FA). Users can use an authenticator app (like Google Authenticator) to generate time-based one-time passwords (TOTPs) for verification.

D. Users need to enter a verification code from email or SMS, whichever has higher priority.

This is another common 2FA method. Users can choose to receive verification codes via email or SMS, and the preferred method can be prioritized.

Why other options are incorrect:

B. Users need to get a security token from a trusted network using Reset My Security Token.

Security tokens are typically used for API access without 2FA enabled. With 2FA enabled, users would not need to use a security token.

C. Users need to download and install an authenticator app on their mobile device.

While this is a common step for setting up 2FA with an authenticator app, it's not a prompt that will happen during the login process.

Additional Considerations:

Data Loader uses the Salesforce API for data import/export, so the "two-factor authentication for API Logins" permission is relevant here.

Users can typically choose their preferred 2FA method from available options.

It's important to communicate the 2FA requirements to users in advance to avoid login issues.

By understanding the different 2FA methods and how they apply to API logins, administrators can effectively secure access to Salesforce data.

194] Correct Answers:

C. Resetting a locked-out user's password automatically unlocks the user's account.

D. After resetting a password, the user may be required to activate their device to successfully log in to Salesforce.

Explanation:

C. Resetting a locked-out user's password automatically unlocks the user's account.

When a user's account is locked due to multiple failed login attempts, resetting the password is the standard procedure to unlock the account and allow the user to log in again.

D. After resetting a password, the user may be required to activate their device to successfully log in to Salesforce.

Depending on the organization's security settings, users might be required to activate their devices after a password reset to enhance security. This is a common practice in many organizations.

Why other options are incorrect:

A. Resetting the password will change the user's password policy.

Resetting a password does not affect the overall password policy of the organization. Password policies are defined at the organizational level and apply to all users.

B. Single sign-on users can reset their own passwords using the forgot password link.

While it's possible for single sign-on (SSO) users to reset their passwords, it depends on the SSO provider's configuration. Not all SSO providers offer this functionality.

By understanding these considerations, the administrator can effectively assist the user in regaining access to Salesforce while maintaining security best practices.

195] Correct Answers:

A. Communities

C. Components

Explanation:

A. Communities: AppExchange offers a wide range of community platforms and tools that can be used to create online communities for customers, partners, or employees. These communities can foster collaboration, knowledge sharing, and customer engagement.

C. Components: AppExchange provides pre-built components like Lightning Web Components, Apex code, and data models that can be used to customize and extend Salesforce functionality without starting from scratch. This saves time and effort in development.

Why other options are incorrect:

B. Consultants: While consultants can be found through AppExchange, they are not a product or solution. Consultants provide services to help organizations implement and customize Salesforce.

D. Customers: Customers are not a product on AppExchange. AppExchange is a marketplace for applications and components, not customers.

By leveraging the power of Communities and Components from AppExchange, administrators can significantly enhance their organization's capabilities and efficiency.

196] Answer: A. Related Lookup Filters

Explanation:

Related Lookup Filters allow you to customize the view of related records on a page layout. This means you can specify which fields are displayed for different user profiles or record types.

In this case, the administrator can create two different related lookup filters for the Case related list on the Account page layout: one for Sales users and another for Customer Care users.

The Sales filter would display Case Created Date and Status fields.

The Customer Care filter would display Owner, Status, and Contact fields.

Why other options are incorrect:

B. Compact Layout Editor: While used for customizing the display of fields on a record page, it doesn't apply to related lists.

C. Page Layout Editor: While used for customizing the overall layout of a record page, it doesn't specifically address differences in related list views for different user groups.

D. Search Layout Editor: This is used for customizing search results, not related list views.

By using Related Lookup Filters, the administrator can effectively tailor the Case information displayed to the specific needs of the Sales and Customer Care teams.

197] Answer: C. Knowledge Articles

Explanation:

Knowledge Articles are a centralized repository for information that can be accessed by both agents and customers.

By creating knowledge articles with the top five troubleshooting tips for common issues, the support team can quickly reference and share this information with customers.

This approach ensures consistency in responses, reduces response time, and empowers customers to potentially resolve issues independently.

Why other options are incorrect:

A. Auto-Response Rules: While auto-response rules can automate initial responses, they are not suitable for providing detailed troubleshooting steps.

B. Email Alerts: Email alerts are primarily used for notifications, not for sharing knowledge or information.

D. Assignment Rules: Assignment rules are used to automatically route cases to specific agents or queues, not for providing information to customers.

By implementing Knowledge Articles, Cloud Kicks can improve customer satisfaction and efficiency in resolving issues.

198] Answer: D. Add the Salesforce Mobile and Lightning Experience action to the page layout.

Explanation:

To make a custom quick action available on the Salesforce mobile app, you need to specifically enable it for mobile. This is achieved by selecting the "Salesforce Mobile and Lightning Experience Action" option when creating or editing the quick action.

Once the action is enabled for mobile, it will automatically appear on the Account record page in the Salesforce mobile app, allowing users to create new cases directly from there.

Why other options are incorrect:

A. Create a custom Lightning App with the action: While Lightning Apps are used to group components for specific user needs, they are not necessary for making a quick action available on mobile.

B. Modify compact Case page layout to include the action: Quick actions are associated with the record they are created from (in this case, Account), not the record they create (Case).

C. Include the action in the Salesforce Mobile Navigation menu: The navigation menu is for top-level navigation, not for actions within a specific record.

By following this approach, the administrator ensures that the custom quick action is accessible and convenient for users on both desktop and mobile devices.

199] Answer: A. Email Notifications

Explanation:

To display an email quick action on the case feed, the Email Notifications feature must be enabled. This setting controls whether email actions are visible in the feed.

While Email-to-Case, Email Alerts, and Email Templates are related to email functionality in Salesforce, they do not directly impact the visibility of an email quick action on the case feed.

By enabling Email Notifications, the administrator can ensure that the email quick action is displayed as expected on the case feed.

200] Answer: A. Activate the critical update in a sandbox.

Explanation:

Always test critical updates in a sandbox environment before deploying to production. This is a fundamental principle of Salesforce administration.

By activating the critical update in a sandbox, the administrator can:

- Assess the update's impact on existing customizations and configurations.
- Identify potential issues or conflicts.
- Test the update's functionality thoroughly.
- Create a backup plan if necessary.
- Once the update has been thoroughly tested and validated in the sandbox, it can then be safely deployed to production.
- Activating a critical update directly in production without testing is highly risky and could lead to unexpected consequences.

201] The administrator needs to automatically create two tasks based on an opportunity's stage: one immediately after closing as won and another 60 days later.

The Correct Answer:

A. Process Builder and B. Workflow Rule

Explanation:

Process Builder and Workflow Rule are the two primary tools for automating tasks in Salesforce based on specific criteria. In this case, we need to create automated actions based on the opportunity stage changing to "Closed Won".

- Process Builder:

Provides a visual interface for creating complex automated processes.

Can handle multiple criteria and actions, making it suitable for complex scenarios.

Ideal for creating the initial task upon closing the opportunity as won.

- Workflow Rule:

Offers a more traditional, rule-based approach to automation.

Simpler to use for straightforward actions.

Well-suited for creating the follow-up task after 60 days, as it involves a time-based trigger.

Why Other Options are Incorrect:

C. Field Update: This tool is used to modify field values based on certain conditions. It doesn't create tasks.

D. Outbound Message: This tool is for sending data to external systems, not for creating internal tasks.

Additional Considerations:

- Task Assignment: Determine who will be assigned to the tasks (opportunity owner, other users, or a queue).
- Task Subject and Description: Define the content of the tasks.
- Task Due Date: Set the due date for the follow-up task (60 days after closing).
- Task Priority: Assign appropriate priority levels to the tasks.
- Email Notifications: Consider sending email notifications to the task owners.
- Testing: Thoroughly test the automation to ensure it works as expected.

By combining Process Builder and Workflow Rule, the administrator can effectively automate the creation of follow-up tasks based on opportunity closure, improving sales team efficiency and customer satisfaction.

Made in the USA
Monee, IL
26 November 2024

71379254R00122